22 Daily Readings from the Book of Colossians

22 DAILY READINGS FROM THE BOOK OF COLOSSIANS

Hold Your Course

Roger Ellsworth

EVANGELICAL PRESS

EVANGELICAL PRESS
Faverdale North Industrial Estate, Darlington, DL3 0PH
England

Evangelical Press USA
PO Box 825, Webster, NY 14580

e-mail: sales@evangelicalpress.org

web: http://www.evangelicalpress.org

British Library Cataloguing in Publication Data available

ISBN 0 85234 592 5

Printed in the United States of America

*The following pages are lovingly dedicated
to Paul and Retha Orrick*

Contents

Day 1
Introduction

- *Read the following chapter*
- *Answer the questions in the section 'For your journal'*

The letter to the Colossians was written by the apostle Paul to believers in the city of Colosse, which was located in the Lycus River valley near the more prominent cities of Laodicea (eleven miles to the northwest) and Hierapolis (fifteen miles to the northwest).

Some deny Paul's authorship because of the presence of words that do not appear in his other epistles (e.g. 'fullness', 'basic principles'). The logical explanation is that the apostle had to use these terms to refute the false arguments of those who regularly employed them.

While Paul never visited Colosse, it is not surprising that he wrote this letter. The church there was a by-product of his three-year ministry in Ephesus (Acts 19:1-20:38). During that ministry two Colossians, Epaphras and Philemon, were brought to the knowledge of the Lord. Aflame with love for Christ, they went home to share the gospel, and the church was born.

Paul was in Ephesus from A.D. 54 to 57. He wrote to the Colossians in A.D. 60 or 61. One of the apostle's 'prison epistles', Colossians was probably written during his first imprisonment in the city of Rome.

The Colossians' need for Paul's letter

What caused the apostle to write this letter? He had evidently received from Epaphras a disturbing report about developments in the church. Paul's letter enables us to piece together some of what had taken place. A man with a charismatic personality had come to the church, acting as something of a spiritual guru and offering the believers there some very desirable benefits. (The 'he' in Colossians 2:18 suggests there was one false teacher. It seems likely, however, that this one teacher had associates. I will be, therefore, referring both to the false teacher and the false teachers).

What system of thought were this teacher and his associates offering the members of the Colossian church? The apostle does not give a formal summary. Its major parts can be reconstructed, however, by looking at the apostle's criticisms of it. Michael Bentley writes: '...as we study this letter, it will be like listening to one side of a telephone conversation. We can get some idea of what the person at the other end of the line is saying by the part of the conversation that we hear.'[1]

What, then, can we conclude about the false teaching in Colosse from listening to Paul's end of the conversation? In general, we can say this teaching was designed to take the Colossians 'beyond apostolic Christianity'.[2]

Did the Colossian believers desire spiritual insights they had never known and a spiritual fullness they had never achieved? This teacher had received special revelations from God and could show them the way!

Were the Colossians tiring of their struggle against the flesh? This teacher could give them very specific rules and regulations for victory! They were to beat down their flesh by having themselves circumcised. They were to practice fasting so they could open their spirits to receiving new and exciting revelations from God. They were to follow the calendar formulated by this man.

In so doing, they would please the higher spirit beings and bring their lives into harmony with them and with the planets and stars. They were, of course, to follow everything this teacher said because his teachings, he asserted, came directly from God through visions and ecstatic experiences.

Were the Colossian believers living in fear of dark and sinister spirits who supposedly controlled every detail of daily living? This teacher could put them in touch with good angels who could counteract the evil beings!

Where did this teacher get these notions? He claimed, as we have noted, that they came from God, but the nature of his teachings indicates that he had functioned as something of a spiritual scavenger, picking up an idea here and another there. The result was a set of teachings that was part Judaism, part paganism and part his own innovation.

We might even have in this particular teacher an early expression of the 'Gnostic' movement that would soon come to prominence and plague so much of early Christianity. The term 'Gnosticism' is derived from the Greek noun 'gnosis' which means 'knowledge'. The Gnostics claimed special enlightenment. They believed that they possessed truth unknown to others, truth which God had directly revealed to them. These people looked upon themselves, therefore, as something of a spiritual aristocracy in the church.

The apostle Paul could not take lightly the report of Epaphras. The Colossian believers lived in a city in which religious blending (syncretism) was the order of the day. In an environment in which it was common to borrow ideas from other religions, Paul could easily see the Colossians uncritically accepting the teachings of the charismatic leader who had come to their church.

The apostle was alarmed because the Colossian believers were not giving indications that they understood where such borrowing would lead. And where was that? Paul's letter makes the answer shine as the noonday sun: away from the Lord Jesus Christ! These new teachings were packaged and presented to the Colossians as a gigantic step forward. Paul wrote to say that they constituted a gigantic step backward. The Colossians already had in Christ everything they needed.

> *Paul picked up his pen, then, with a sense of tremendous urgency, to issue a ringing call to the Colossians to see the sufficiency of Christ. The Colossians had to understand that the more they exalted the teachings of this religious guru, the more they diminished the Lord Jesus Christ. They could not have it both ways. They had to see that the effect of this new teaching was to give Christ a place but not the supreme place. But Christ claims the supreme place, and when he is not given that place he has no place at all.*

An overview of Paul's letter

While the apostle was eager to address the situation threatening the church, he does not come out with both fists flying. He first warmly greets the church (1:1-2), expresses thanks to God (1:3-8) for them and offers a prayer for them (1:9-14). He then moves to the main part of his letter in which he emphatically declares the supremacy and sufficiency of Christ and applies these to the false teaching confronting the church (1:15-2:23). The key texts in this section are as follows:

- '...that in all things He may have the pre-eminence' (1:18)

- '...it pleased the Father that in Him all the fullness should dwell' (1:19)

• 'For in Him dwells all the fullness of the Godhead bodily; and you are complete in Him, who is the head of all principality and power' (2:9-10)

The last part of the letter is a plea for the Colossians to reflect the supremacy of Christ in every aspect of their lives (3:1-4:6). This is followed by concluding greetings and exhortations (4:7-18).

Our need for Paul's letter

While every book of the Bible has constant and on-going validity for the church of the Lord Jesus Christ, there are times in which she more urgently needs the teachings of some. Colossians is in that special category of books that are vitally needed and immensely relevant. The reasons are:

• This is a time in which many do not recognize Christianity as a body of revealed truth. It is rather a day in which people feel free to carry into their Christian faith various teachings and notions that they picked up here and there. Many seem to regard Christianity as something that is still under construction. We have all seen these words on the box of something we purchased: SOME ASSEMBLY REQUIRED. We often come across teachings that give the impression that Christianity is still in need of assembly, that it is not 'the faith once delivered to the saints' (Jude 3).

• This is a day in which Christian 'Gnosticism' runs rampant. Many believers live on the basis of 'God has shown this to me' or 'God has revealed that to me'. On the basis of supposed special revelation from God, they do not hesitate to set aside the clear teachings of Scripture.

• Our age is also one in which the Lord Jesus Christ is being minimized. It would not seem to be the case. The Name of Jesus is splashed across our songs and sermons. But is the Jesus who is so prominently mentioned the Christ of the Bible? Is he supreme and worthy of supreme allegiance? Or do we distribute supremacy among the Lord Jesus and the angels? Angel pins and figurines are everywhere, and many talk easily about feeling more comfortable with angels than God. Some glowingly refer to praying to their angel.

It is so easy to minimize the Lord Jesus without even realizing that we are doing so. Many songs we sing use his Name, but they are really more about our feelings and our experiences than they are about him.

We minimize Christ when, out of fear that we will offend others or be considered intolerant, we do not hold to the full truth about him. The world will let us have Jesus if we will allow them to do surgery on him. They want to remove his deity, that is, his divine nature. Such people say he was an unusual man, but just a man. He could not possibly have been God in human flesh. They want to remove his sinlessness, alleging that he committed sins just as every other man! They want to remove his redeeming death on the cross, especially that aspect of him receiving the wrath of God in the stead of sinners. And, oh, how they want to remove the finality of Christ! They cannot tolerate any teaching that Jesus Christ is the only way of salvation.

When we receive our Christ back from the surgeons, we immediately see we have a very small Christ indeed, one that bears no resemblance at all to the mighty Christ set forth in the pages of God's Word.

• This is also a time in which many Christians are look-ing for some sort of formula that will give them a spiritual fullness which they have not known before.

These symptoms of the Colossian disease mean we need to take the medicine of Paul's letter.

For your journal...

1. Write down any evidences you see that the church today is di-minishing Christ. What can you do to combat this trend?

2. Reflect on what Christ has done for you. Jot down ways in which you can show your gratitude.

Colossians 1:2b

*Grace to you and peace
from God our Father and the Lord Jesus Christ*

Day 2
Affection for the Church

- Begin by reading Colossians 1:1-5
- Pray about what you have read
- Make notes on what you think God is teaching you
- Read the following chapter
- Answer the questions in the 'For your journal' section

The apostle introduces his letter by warmly greeting the Colossians (vv. 1-2) and by expressing thanks to God for them (vv. 3-8). These verses give us insight into the heart of this great man. He was not a mean-spirited fellow who was eager for a fight. He was rather a pastor who was genuinely concerned for the spiritual welfare of his people. Although he had not visited Colosse, the apostle Paul had a sincere interest in the progress of the gospel there. He was a gospel-centred man. Anything having to do with the gospel was to him of intense interest and immense importance.

Every child of God is interested in the work of the gospel. The question is to what degree. The church has a desperate need for passionate lovers of the gospel of Christ who have hearts for the whole world. She is in a lamentable state when she has 'worldly members' instead of 'world-hearted members'.

Warm greetings (vv. 1-2)

Paul identifies himself

Paul was 'an apostle of Jesus Christ' (v. 1). The word 'apostle' means 'messenger'. To be an apostle of Christ was, therefore, to be sent by him as his ambassador. An apostle was not just an ancient equivalent of today's preacher or pastor. Many these days are quick to find fault with their preachers and disagree with their preaching. This happens because everyone agrees that preachers are fallible. But an apostle was a special emissary of the Lord Jesus Christ and carried special authority. There were false apostles, but a true apostle spoke with the authority of Christ himself.

It was customary for Paul to open his letters with a reference to his apostleship (Rom. 1:1; 1 Cor. 1:1; 2 Cor. 1:1; Gal. 1:1; Eph. 1:1; 1 Tim. 1:1; 2 Tim. 1:1; Titus 1:1). The Colossians had to understand that he was writing with authority. He was not writing to merely offer his opinions or to make suggestions.

Paul's apostleship meant that the Colossians should read his letter as the Lord Jesus speaking to them. It was Christ himself who would call them to Christ-centredness. We show that we understand apostleship if we accept the writings of the apostles as the Word of God without quarrelling with their teachings.

Paul's apostleship was also 'by the will of God'. It could be no other way. What comes through Christ as its agent must also come from God as its source. There is no division between the Father and the Son.

Paul's claim to authority is made more plain and powerful by his reference to Timothy. The apostle was glad to acknowledge Timothy as a brother, and happy to include him in his greeting, but he did not call him an apostle. This was not egotism on the part of Paul. It was rather God's will.

The apostle's mention of the widely-known and much-appreciated Timothy, who was with him at the time, also showed that he completely endorsed the forthcoming indictment of the Colossian heresy.

Paul addresses his readers

Paul calls the Colossians 'saints'. The word refers to those whom God had chosen and set apart for himself. The Colossians had been set apart by God; they were delivered from sin and sanctified to God and his purpose for them. This constituted both an enormous privilege and a solemn responsibility.

They were also 'faithful brethren in Christ'. Brothers share a special kinship by virtue of their common origin or common life, and the apostle, Christ-centred man that he was, leaves no doubt about the source of the common life among Christians. It is 'in Christ'. All those who are in Christ are also 'faithful'. No, they are not perfect, but, while they sometimes waver and falter, the desire of their hearts and the general tenor of their lives is that of steadfast devotion to Christ.

Although the Colossians were being threatened by an insidious teaching, the apostle thought the best regarding them. The fact they were so threatened and tempted had not diminished or tarnished his regard for them. This man so full of love for Christ could not help but be full of warmth and tenderness towards those who belonged to Christ.

Paul's inclusion of his usual wish for grace and peace does not allow us to take it as an empty formality. The man was much too earnest regarding spiritual matters to allow for such a thing – and much too concerned about the spiritual well-being of his readers! He sincerely desired that the Colossians would experience both 'grace' and 'peace'.

They had, of course, already experienced the grace of God in conversion, but the Christian life from beginning to end is one long drink from the fountain of grace. With the word 'grace', Paul was expressing his desire that God would be pleased to pour his rich blessings into their lives, and that they would be mindful that he was doing so. 'Peace' is, of course, the result of grace. Paul would have them enjoying the calm tranquillity that comes from knowing that the grace of God was at work in them and for them.

Both grace and peace come from 'God our Father' as their source and from 'the Lord Jesus Christ' as their channel or as the means through which they are conveyed to believers.

Paul's opening words show a great deal of tenderness and kindness. He knew there were true believers at Colosse, and he knew that fellow-believers are always to be treated with Christian kindness. The believers in Colosse were flawed in many ways, but the apostle still showed them the tenderness of Christ. We do well in these days in which doctrinal error abounds to emulate him. We must stand for the truth, but we must stand for it with the beauty and winsomeness of the Lord Jesus himself. Let us not give one inch in being Christ-centred, but let us also prove our Christ-centredness by being Christ-like.

Heartfelt thanksgiving (vv. 3-5)

To God (v. 3)

Paul's thanksgiving for the Colossians was directed to God. This constitutes a ringing affirmation that his readers could take absolutely no credit for their standing with God. Salvation from top to bottom is the work of God.

The God to whom Paul gave thanks is 'the God and Father of our Lord Jesus Christ'. The phrase is probably more accurately rendered 'to God, the Father of our Lord Jesus Christ'.

What mystery! The God to whom the apostle expressed thanks is the Father of the second person of the Trinity. John Gill writes: 'Christ is the Son of God, not by creation, nor by adoption, nor by office, but by nature; he is the true, proper, natural, and eternal Son of God'.[1]

God is the Father of 'our Lord Jesus Christ'. A large creed is packed into those words! The second person of the Trinity took unto himself humanity and came in the person of Jesus of Nazareth. But Jesus, while fully man, was much more. He was at one and the same time fully God, the Sovereign Lord of Glory, who was sent by God as the Christ, that is, the Messiah.

It may be going too far to suggest that the apostle chose these words of greeting as a way of firing a shot across the bow of the ship of heresy sailing through the Colossian waters, a heresy that diminished Christ. These are words that were as natural to Paul as his breathing. This was his faith and his passion. It did not take heresy to call from Paul expressions of warm-hearted devotion to God the Father and Christ the Son.

Through prayer (v. 3)

Paul's thanksgiving was not just something he felt within. It was openly expressed in consistent prayer. The phrase 'praying always for you' doesn't mean that he did nothing but pray. It rather means that he never failed to include the Colossians when he prayed.

We readily admit that the apostle Paul was an extraordinary man, one of the greatest in history. We must also understand that he was a man of prayer. We must connect the dots. In other words, we must not try to explain the greatness of the man apart from his prayer life.

For faith and love (v. 4)

Paul and Timothy had heard from Epaphras about the 'faith' of the believers in Colosse (v. 7). The fact that Paul thanked God for it tells us that it was the gift of God (Eph. 2:8-9). The faith which God had given was 'in Christ Jesus', that is, it moved in the sphere of the one whom God had appointed and anointed to perform the work of redemption.

The apostle was also thankful for their 'love for all the saints'. Where faith in Christ is found, love for his people will inevitably be found. The two can no more be separated than the sun and its rays. While there is certainly a universal quality to this love, that is, an interest in and love for Christians everywhere, it is likely that Paul was here referring to the Colossians' love for all their number without regard to class or standing.

The apostle Paul is well known for mentioning faith, hope and love together (1 Cor. 13:13; Gal. 5:5-6; 1 Thess. 1:3), but here they are not equivalent virtues that are produced by the gospel. It is rather the hope that produces the faith and love. The Colossians had the faith and love because they had heard about and embraced the hope.

Therefore, the hope is not the subjective feeling of eager anticipation for heaven but rather the objective reality of heaven itself.

This hope, Paul says, 'is laid up for you in heaven'. It is that which God has laid by and is holding in reserve for all his people (1 Peter 1:4).

For your journal...

1. The tenderness Paul manifests in his opening words should cause us to think of the tenderness of Jesus. Leaf through one of the four gospels. Jot down as many examples as you can of his tenderness.

2. What are some of the reasons you are thankful for your own church?

3. Read 1 Peter 1:3-5. What does this passage say about the inheritance God is reserving for his people?

Colossians 1:5b

...of which you heard before in the word of the truth of the gospel...

Day 3
Thanksgiving for the Gospel

- *Begin by reading Colossians 1:5-8*
- *Pray about what you have read*
- *Make notes on what you think God is teaching you*
- *Read the following chapter*
- *Answer the questions in the 'For your journal' section*

In these verses the apostle Paul continues his prayer of thanksgiving to God for the Colossians. He was thankful for their faith and their love, both of which had been produced by hope. How did they come to have this hope? It had come from and through the gospel of Christ.

Here, then, is the sequence: In order to be thankful for their faith and love, Paul had to be thankful for their hope; and in order to be thankful for their hope, Paul had to be thankful for the gospel. The gospel gave Paul much for which to be thankful, but at this point, he contents himself with mentioning only some of those things.

The truth of the gospel (v. 5)

The gospel is a sure and reliable word. It is not a human invention or the product of human speculation. The gospel of God (1

Thess. 2:9) has to be a true gospel because God is a God of truth and cannot lie (Titus 1:2; Heb. 6:18).

As far as many are concerned, it is almost impossible to define the gospel. They contend that it means one thing to one person and something quite different to another, and both views are equally valid. The Apostle Paul would have none of this. The Christians of Colosse were saved because they had heard a clear and distinct message, a message that was true. Paul says they had heard 'the word of truth of the gospel' (v. 5). This is also a message that they had 'learned' (v. 7). The idea here is that a body of truth had been delivered to them, and they had applied themselves to understanding it. Paul disputes the notion that the gospel is an unclear and undefinable thing. There is, then, a distinct gospel message to be understood and declared.

The spreading of the gospel (v. 6)

The fact that the gospel had found its way to Colosse was to Paul another evidence that it was making progress 'in all the world'. No, Paul was not giving way here to wishful thinking. The pace of the gospel was indeed brisk at that time. William Hendriksen writes: 'The rapid progress of the gospel in the early days has ever been the amazement of the historian.'[1]

Hendriksen proceeds to offer this observation from Justin Martyr, who wrote in the middle of the second century: 'There is no people, Greek or barbarian, or of any other race, by whatever appellation or manners they may be distinguished, however ignorant of arts or agriculture, whether they dwell in tents or wander about in covered wagons, among whom prayers and thanksgivings are not offering in the name of the crucified Jesus to the Father and Creator of all things.'[2]

Hendriksen also quotes the church father Tertullian, who says of Christians: 'We are but of yesterday, and yet we already fill your cities, islands, camps, your palace, senate, and forum. We have left you only your temples.'[3]

The power of the gospel (v. 6)

The mere fact that the pace of the gospel was so brisk did not prove anything. Even false messages can have winged feet. But the gospel carried with it the power to produce fruit, that is, true spiritual results. This fruit was evident in the lives of the Colossians themselves.

Because the Colossians had heard the gospel, Paul had heard about them (v. 8). The gospel, where it is truly heard and received, does not leave people the same. It makes a difference.

The gospel carries with it the power of God to change lives, and wherever it is genuinely embraced a change of conduct takes place. If such a change is missing, it is not because of any deficiency in the gospel but rather because it has only been outwardly professed but not inwardly received.

The grace of the gospel (v. 6)

Those who do receive the gospel, as had the Colossians, know 'the grace of God in truth.'

Salvation is entirely a matter of God's grace. It is not part God's doing and part ours. It is the result of God having chosen his people in eternity, having given them spiritual life and having called them to himself in repentance and faith. This grace operates in and through God's truth. The two are married and can never be divorced. God's truth is, of course, revealed in his word which sets forth his divine and holy nature, the sinfulness of mankind, the certainty of judgement, the redeeming work of the Lord Jesus Christ and the application of that work to individuals by the Holy Spirit.

The preaching of the gospel (vv. 7-8)

God uses human instruments to channel his grace to unbelievers. In the case of the Colossians, he had used Epaphras, whom Paul describes as 'our dear fellow servant' and 'a faithful minister of Christ'. These terms tell us three things about Paul:

1. He was a man of such a large and generous spirit that he treasured with genuine affection those who laboured with him in the cause of Christ.

2. He regarded gospel ministers as slaves of Christ, that is, having no will of their own but existing for the sole purpose of carrying out the desires of their master. The apostle would contend with those who consider his words to lean too much towards self-deprecation. In his slavery he found life's highest freedom and its greatest privilege because his slavery was to the best of all masters, the Lord Jesus Christ, who had loved him and died for him.

3. He regarded faithfulness as the sine qua non of ministry. The faithful ministry of Epaphras had brought blessing to the Colossians. The false teachers in their midst who refused to be faithful to Christ could bring nothing but heartache and ruin.

On whose behalf had Epaphras ministered? Some versions have 'on your behalf' (e.g. New King James Version) and others 'on our behalf' (e.g. New American Standard Bible).

If the former is correct, Paul was saying that Epaphras had ministered to him and to Timothy on behalf of the Colossians.

This would have occurred when Epaphras came to Rome to report about developments among the Colossians and to express their love for the apostle and Timothy.

If the latter is correct, Paul was asserting that Epaphras had stepped in and preached the gospel to the Colossians on behalf of Timothy and himself, neither of whom was able to go there. This interpretation fits nicely with the words 'you also learned from Epaphras' (v. 7).

Epaphras was a faithful minister, then, because he had declared the gospel to the Colossians on behalf of Paul and Timothy. But Paul further commends him as the one 'who also declared to us your love in the Spirit'.

Something of the marvel of the gospel stands out in Epaphras' declaration of the Colossians' love for Paul and Timothy. Charles R. Erdman explains: 'It was not the love which springs from personal acquaintance and friendship, such as was felt for Paul by the Philippians. It was that sympathy and affection which the Holy Spirit inspires toward those who have never seen one another in the flesh but who share a common faith and hope centering upon Christ.'[4]

It is to be expected that Paul, having already mentioned the Father and the Son, would include a reference to the Holy Spirit. The fact that this is his only such mention in Colossians should not be taken to mean that the Holy Spirit was not prominent in his thinking.

Paul's thanksgiving for the Colossians prompted Charles Spurgeon to write:

> *For the church that was at Colosse, Paul gave hearty thanks to God for many most important blessings, especially for their faith, their love, and their hope. It would be a very useful exercise to our hearts if we would often give thanks to God for*

*the gifts and graces which we discover in our Christian breth-
ren. I am afraid we are more inclined to spy out their faults,
and to suppose that we deplore them, than we are to discern
the work of the Holy Spirit in them, and from the bottom of
our hearts to give thanks to God for them.*[5]

For your journal...

1. What is your response to the points of this chapter?

2. Write a paragraph or two about a pastor whose ministry was
   particularly used of God to help you. Be sure to thank God for
   faithful pastors.

Colossians 1:9a

For this reason we also, since the day we heard it, do not cease to pray for you...

Day 4
A Prayer for Intercession

- *Begin by reading Colossians 1:9-11*
- *Pray about what you have read*
- *Make notes on what you think God is teaching you*
- *Read the following chapter*
- *Answer the questions in the 'For your journal' section*

In verse 3, the apostle introduced two matters. First, he indicated that he wanted to give thanks for the Colossians. Secondly, he mentioned his praying for them. After introducing these points, he takes each in order. We have his thanksgiving expressed in verses 3 through 8. In the verses before us, we have his prayer.

Prayer of any kind is very difficult and demanding business, but praying for others may very well be the most difficult of all. How we struggle with this! How easy it is to find ourselves wondering what we should ask! Our difficulty at this point often drives us to simply ask God to 'bless' the person for whom we are praying.

Paul was far more specific — and spiritual! — in his praying for the Colossians.

Charles Spurgeon calls us to intercession by writing:

Paul felt encouraged by what he saw in the Colossian believers to pray for God to enrich them yet further. It should be our desire that our best brethren should be better, and that those who are most like Jesus should be still more completely conformed to His image. We cannot more wisely show our love to our friends than by first acknowledging the grace which is in them, and then by praying that God may give them more.[1]

We should note that the apostle refers to praying and asking ('to pray for you, and to ask'). The asking aspect reminds us that we pray not to inform God or to explain anything to him. We come to God as humble and helpless people who are totally dependent upon his grace and who have absolutely no other resource.

William Hendriksen distinguishes between praying and asking in this way: 'Praying is the more general and comprehensive term. It indicates any form of reverent address directed to the Deity, whether we "take hold of God" by means of intercession, supplication, adoration, or thanksgiving. Asking is more specific. It refers to making definite, humble requests.'[2]

While asking implies helplessness on the part of the one doing it, those believers who ask may do so with firm confidence, remembering the words of the Lord Jesus: 'Ask, and it will be given to you; seek, and you will find; knock, and it will be opened to you. For everyone who asks receives, and he who seeks finds, and to him who knocks it will be opened' (Matt. 7:7-8).

Paul's prayer consists of two major petitions, each of which is signalled by the word 'that' in the New King James Version. First, he prays 'that' they 'may be filled with the knowledge of His will.'

The knowledge of God's will (v. 9)

This is understanding how God wants his people to live. A.W. Pink calls it 'the knowledge of God's will as it respects the ordering of our daily walk in the world.'[3]

Hendriksen writes of this knowledge: 'It is not the kind of mysterious gnosis which teachers of the gnostic type claimed for their "initiates." On the contrary, it is penetrating insight into God's wonderful, redemptive revelation in Jesus Christ, a discernment with fruits for practical life'.[4]

To 'be filled' with this knowledge is, in the word of R.C.H. Lenski, to have 'no gaps in this knowledge' that will leave the readers 'open to deception.' Lenski continues: 'They are to know fully "his (God's) will" so that no one may substitute something for what God has really willed.'[5]

The word 'wisdom' essentially refers to knowing how to live. It is knowing how to respond to what life throws at us. We might liken it to driving a car. As we drive along, we are confronted by all sorts of things. Another driver pulls out in front of us or a huge chuck hole suddenly appears, and to avoid a wreck we must respond quickly and appropriately.

We are all called upon to drive the car of life, and as we go down the road of life we encounter many challenges. Wisdom means we respond appropriately. It is making the right choices in life. How often lives are wrecked by lack of wisdom!

With the words 'spiritual understanding' Paul makes this point: the wisdom we need for living comes from understanding spiritual truths.

And where do we find spiritual truths? The false teachers in Colosse suggested that such truths came through direct enlightenment from God. They were very fond of saying 'God told me' and 'God revealed this to me.' Such phrases were their stock in trade.

The problem with this kind of thing is that self so easily gets in the way. When we seek to drive the car of life by depending on truths that God reveals directly to us, we have a tendency to hear what we want to hear. How often God agrees with us!

Where, then, are we to look for spiritual truths? The apostle Paul would have us to turn to the Word of God. He will later write: 'Let the word of Christ dwell in you richly' (Col. 3:16).

Here, then, is the sequence: As we drive along life's way, we are faced with challenges that require wise choices, choices we can make if we have spiritual understanding, and we get spiritual understanding from the Word of God.

Paul's emphasis on spiritual understanding underscores for us the importance of taking in the Word of God through personal reading and study and through the public services of the church. Nothing is more important. Sometimes it may seem that we are not receiving much benefit from the intake of God's Word. But a heavy intake of God's Word produces benefits of which we are not even aware.

When a driver is suddenly confronted with a situation that requires a quick response, he does not have time to pull over to the side and take out his driving manual. He has to respond, and he is able to respond because of the understanding he has built up over the years.

When we Christians are confronted with the crises of life, we will be able to respond in the appropriate and wise way if we have through time built up our spiritual understanding by studying the Word of God.

A pleasing walk (vv. 10-12)

The apostle now adds a second petition on behalf of the Colossians, namely, that have 'a walk worthy of the Lord, fully pleasing Him' (v. 10).

The word 'walk' refers to conduct, behaviour or way of life.
This is to be in a manner that is 'worthy of the Lord,' that is, in
a way which corresponds to the person of Christ and the saving
work which he has done for his people. This walking is also to
be done in a manner that is 'fully pleasing' to the Lord. We are
to live with the awareness of the Lord's awareness. He sees every
act, hears every word and knows every thought, and he is either
pleased or displeased. Being conscious of this, the saints of God
should seek to act, speak and think only in ways that please the
Lord. He who was 'pleased' to bruise his Son (Isa. 53:10) on behalf of his people should be pleased by his people.

The term 'walk' also reminds us that Christians are on a journey. By the grace of God, they have been made citizens of heaven
(Phil. 3:20). They are now in the process of travelling from this
perishing, sinful world to that perfect world. As they travel, they
are conscious that they are on display, that they are being observed by those who have not yet taken up the journey. It is vital,
therefore, for Christians to travel in the right way, in a way that
is in keeping with the Lord who made them his subjects. They
desire as they travel life's pathway to make it abundantly clear
that their Lord is the best of all masters, that their new citizenship is the best of all blessings and that travelling worthily is the
best of all privileges.

While Christians are travelling to a perfect world, they themselves will not be perfect until they get there. The vile world
through which they are now travelling is not , in the words of
Isaac Watts, 'a friend to grace' to help them 'on to God'.[6] As
believers make their way along they find no shortage of things to
slow their progress and to put them off their feet. The world is
filled with evil enticements to stain Christian character and dev-
ilish doctrines to cloud Christian thinking. Yielding to either or
both constitutes unworthy walking. And any episode of unworthy walking makes the believer smart with pain that he or she
could repay such a worthy Lord with such unworthy behaviour.

Because he was so keenly aware of the unrelenting danger of the world, Paul found it urgently necessary to pray for the Colossians to walk worthily and pleasingly.

But the apostle could not be content to state the matter generally. He knew human nature. We all suffer from this tendency to define spiritual things for ourselves. We come up with the definition, and, voila!, we live up to our definition.

Paul knew that it would be very easy for his readers to read his words and say: 'I think I am walking in a worthy manner!' Knowing this tendency, he proceeded to specify four components of living in a worthy manner, the last of which we shall examine in the next chapter.

Being fruitful in every good work (v. 10)

First, Christians walk in a fitting and worthy manner by 'being fruitful,' that is by producing fruit. The fruit they are to produce is 'every good work.'

Generally speaking, anything the Christian does to conform to the will of God as it is expressed in Scripture constitutes a good work.

We should all be absolutely convinced that it is impossible for us to be saved by good works. Salvation is entirely a matter of grace. We are saved by grace through faith, and not by good works (Eph. 2:8-9). We must also be absolutely convinced that it is equally impossible to be saved and not produce good works. While good works are not the source of salvation, they are certainly the result of it. We might say they are not the root of salvation but the fruit of it.

Because no Christian maintains good works to the degree that he should, Paul prayed that the Colossians would increase in this area. His desire that they be fruitful 'in every good work' tells us not to think we are pleasing God only when we can point to success in one or two areas of our Christian walk. We are rather to vigorously pursue the life that abounds in all spiritual graces.

Increasing in the knowledge of God (v. 10)

Furthermore, God's people walk in a worthy and pleasing manner when they are 'increasing in the knowledge of God.'

William Hendriksen writes: 'Note that the apostle makes the clear knowledge of God both the starting point (verse 9) and the resulting characteristic (verse 10) of the God-pleasing life. This is not strange: true, experiential knowledge of God brings about an ever-increasing measure of this very commodity.'[7]

Paul wanted the Colossians to be dissatisfied with what they had attained in the area of knowledge of God. There is always more to know about God, and the more we know, the more worthy we walk and the more pleasing we are to God.

Paul was not asking something for the Colossians which he himself did not fervently desire. Although he had walked with the Lord for a number of years, Paul, earnestly yearned to know the Lord better. We find the cry of his heart in his letter to the Philippians: ' ...that I may know Him' (Phil. 3:10).

Strengthened with all might (v. 11)

Here we have the third element of the worthy and pleasing life, namely, 'strengthened with all might'. Life requires great strength, and we do not possess it. But God has 'glorious power', and he graciously gives strength to his weak people (Isa. 40:29).

Through physical weakness, Paul himself had learned that the Lord provides strength for his people (2 Cor. 12:1-9).

How do we know that we have the strength of the Lord? Will we go about churning out miracles? Paul says God's strength manifests itself in 'patience and longsuffering with joy'.

Patience is that quality which enables us to endure adversity and difficulty. To be longsuffering is to suffer long. It means we put up with exasperating conduct and provocative behaviour on the part of others without flying into a rage or seeking revenge.

Worthy living requires more than endurance which can amount to nothing more than a stoical tolerance or resignation that is stubbornly determined to not let others see us 'sweat.' The word 'joy' makes it plain that living worthily requires the Christian to positively embrace these qualities. There can be no doubt that living this way requires strength beyond our own, strength from above. As we seek and find this strength from the Lord and as we put it into practice, we can be confident that our Lord is pleased.

Paul's prayer for fruitfulness, increased knowledge of God, spiritual strength and thanksgiving gives us insight into the premium which the apostle placed on spiritual matters. It also searches – and pinches! – us. Do these things occupy a high enough place in our thinking that we are consistently asking God to grant them to us? How easy it is to lose our way in praying by focusing our petitions on lesser things! And what about praying for others? Are we engaging this on a regular and on-going basis? When we engage in intercession, do we give priority to praying for the same things which Paul asked for the Colossians?

For your journal...

1. Think about your prayer life. How much of it is devoted to intercession? Make a list of those for whom you should be praying. If you already have such a list, try to expand it.

2. Spiritual wisdom results from a heavy intake of Scripture. Do an inventory of your Bible intake. What can you do to increase it?

3. Look again at the three components of a pleasing 'walk' we have covered. Write down ways in which you can improve in each of these areas.

Colossians 1:12

...giving thanks to the Father who has qualified us to be partakers of the inheritance of the saints in light.

Day 5
Thanksgiving for Salvation

- Begin by reading Colossians 1:12-14
- Pray about what you have read
- Make notes on what you think God is teaching you
- Read the following chapter
- Answer the questions in the 'For your journal' section

Here the apostle adds the final of his four components for living in a worthy and pleasing manner: 'giving thanks to the Father'.

Charles Erdman is surely right to observe: 'The very designation of God by the name "Father" might well awaken a spirit of gratitude. It points to the loving Source from which comes "every good and perfect gift."'[1]

The major thing for which Christians are to be thankful is, of course, their salvation. The joy for facing life's hardships can only come from a heart that has been diligently schooled in redemption's work. It cannot be stressed too strongly that Paul addresses thanksgiving for the Colossians' salvation exclusively to God. Not a shred of credit is given to the Colossians themselves. The reason is that salvation is entirely of God. Jean Daille says of salvation: 'This wholly appertainth unto God.'[2]

John Newton celebrates the same truth with these words:

'Twas grace that taught my heart to fear,
And grace my fears relieved.
How precious did that grace appear
The hour I first believed!

Paul could have told the Colossians to be thankful for their salvation and left it at that. But he always found it quite diffi-cult to merely mention salvation. Once he rubbed up against the topic, he invariably found himself glorying in it. He does so here by using five exhilarating phrases (vv. 12-14).

There is no greater or more common failing these days than failing to truly glory in salvation. Pondering carefully Paul's phrases will go a long way toward keeping us from this failure.

Qualified (v. 12)

First, he says the Father '...has qualified us to be partakers of the inheritance of the saints in the light.'

R.C.H. Lenski happily translates 'qualified us' as 'sufficiented us.'[3] The inheritance of the saints in light begins in this life and culminates in heaven. The apostle is telling us that God first fits us to share the lot or portion of the saints in this life. This portion is 'in the light.' Believers, like everyone else, came into this world in a state of spiritual darkness, but God in grace has called them out of that darkness 'into His marvellous light' (1 Peter 2:9).

Paul is repeating to the Colossians that which he affirmed to the Ephesians: 'For you were once darkness, but now you are light in the Lord. Walk as children of light' (Eph. 5:8).

The children of light will finally enter the kingdom of light described by the apostle John in these words: 'And the city had no need of the sun or of the moon to shine in it, for the glory of God illuminated it, and the Lamb is its light. And the nations of those who are saved shall walk in its light, and the kings of the earth bring their glory and honour into it. Its gates shall not be shut at all by day (there shall be no night there)' (Rev. 21:23-25).

The children of light will enter there only because they have been qualified by the Lord. We are sinners by nature. We have the darkness of sin in us and with us and, therefore, cannot enjoy the light that God has prepared in eternity. In order to be partakers of God's inheritance in light we have to be perfectly righteous, and we have no righteousness. Furthermore, there is absolutely nothing we can do to provide it. But – wonderful news! – God himself qualifies sinners to be partakers of the light of glory. In his Son, Jesus Christ, God provided the righteousness that he demands of us and he applies that righteousness to each believer.

We could not be qualified for heaven without it, but with it we can take as our own the words of Count Zinzendorf:

Jesus, Thy blood and righteousness
My beauty are, my glorious dress;
'Midst flaming worlds, in these arrayed,
With joy shall I lift up my head.

Bold shall I stand in Thy great day;
For who aught to my charge shall lay?
Fully through Thee absolved I am
From sin and fear, from guilt and shame.

Delivered (v. 13)

In the second place, thanksgiving is due to God because 'He has delivered us from the power of darkness'.

We all come into this world as part of Satan's kingdom. Oh, the darkness of this kingdom! It is the darkness of ignorance. The citizens of this kingdom have their minds blinded so they cannot see their true condition (2 Cor. 4:3-4). It is the darkness of death. Those who stay in this kingdom will eventually be enveloped by eternal death (2 Peter 2:17; Jude 12-13).

Believers are to rejoice because they have been taken out of this kingdom by the Lord Jesus Christ. Through his redeeming death on the cross, he decisively defeated Satan and delivered all believers from his kingdom of darkness.

While the apostle has not yet mentioned the 'basic principles of the world' (2:8,20), he has already shown the folly of devotion to these spiritual beings. Christ has qualified his people for heaven, and no one, including these spirit-beings, can disqualify them. Christ has delivered his people from the domain of darkness, and no one can reclaim them.

Translated (v. 13)

The third of Paul's glorious phrases is '...and translated us into the kingdom of the Son of His love'.

This phrase refers to the practice of removing people from one country and settling them as colonists in another. How big is salvation? It amounts to nothing less than a change of kingdoms. It takes us out of Satan's kingdom and re-settles us as citizens of God's kingdom. It would have been unspeakably glorious for God to do the former. How astonishing that he would go so far as to do the latter!

The new kingdom in which believers are settled is 'the kingdom of the Son of His love.' This tells us how very certain believers can be of their new citizenship. God loves his Son with an immeasurable and indestructible love. Those who are in Christ can rest assured that this same love is extended to them.

Because of this transfer from one kingdom to another, each believer can say a hearty 'Amen!' to the words of Paul to the Philippians: 'For our citizenship is in heaven, from which we also eagerly wait for the Savior, the Lord Jesus Christ, who will transform our lowly body that it may be conformed to His glorious body, according to the working by which He is able even to subdue all things to Himself' (Phil. 3:20-21).

Redeemed (v. 14)

Paul's fourth phrase is: '...in whom we have redemption through His blood' (v. 14).

The word 'redeemed' means 'to buy back.' Although believers belonged to God by virtue of creation, they were all taken prisoner by sin and held by the chain of God's law. That law demands that the sinner be punished with eternal separation from God.

Believers, however, have been redeemed by the blood of Christ, that is, by the death of Christ. On the cross, Jesus received the eternal separation his people deserve. The law of God was, therefore, satisfied and they were freed. God paid the ransom for them through the death of his Son.

Forgiven (v. 14)

The last of Paul's glorious phrases is 'the forgiveness of sins'. The word 'forgiven' means 'to send away' or 'to cancel a debt'. Satan would have us believe that our sins constitute an insurmountable barrier to entering heaven. He points to those sins and says: 'Look at them! You are not fit to enter heaven!'

But we do not fear a creditor pointing to a statement if that statement has stamped on it these words: PAID IN FULL. And Christians need not fear Satan pointing to their sin debt because Jesus paid it in full.

Qualified! Delivered! Transferred! Redeemed! Forgiven! If we do not feel joyful astonishment over salvation, it must in large measure be due to failing to ponder what these words convey about what we were in sin and what we are in Christ.

> Paul's emphasis on thanksgiving speaks pointedly about our general demeanour, the way in which we 'carry' ourselves. We all have our difficulties and our burdens, but we should never allow these things to obscure our blessings. How blessed we are! Let us, then, go along life's way with our hearts rejoicing and with our mouths filled with thanksgiving. Sour Christians are not walking in a worthy manner and are not pleasing to the Lord.

For your journal...

1. Write a prayer of thanksgiving to God for the salvation that he has provided.

2. The Bible's vocabulary of salvation is very rich. Jot down some salvation concepts not used by Paul in this passage. What do these words mean?

Colossians 1:18b

...that in all things He may have the preeminence

Day 6
The Supremacy of Christ

- *Begin by reading Colossians 1:15-18*
- *Pray about what you have read*
- *Make notes on what you think God is teaching you*
- *Read the following chapter*
- *Answer the questions in the 'For your journal' section*

No one can adequately explain these verses. Their truths are too deep and too sublime for the human mind. Warren Wiersbe says of them: 'Probably no paragraph in the New Testament contains more concentrated doctrine about Jesus Christ than this one.'[1]

These verses require us, therefore, to think about the greatest of all truths regarding the greatest of all persons. Who is sufficient for this? We are all out of our element here.

With these verses Paul begins to grapple very closely with the heretical teachings that were affecting the church of Colosse. Here he dispenses with the preliminaries and engages the enemy in hand-to-hand combat.

There are many who do not like such talk. They hold the view that all beliefs are equally valid and no one can say one is right and another wrong. They would charge Paul with being negative and intolerant. But Paul knew — and we should all know — that there is no room for neutrality when it comes to the Lord Jesus Christ. The word 'Lord' is enough to tell us that. He is either Lord of all or he is not Lord at all. If he is Lord, it is nothing less than spiritual treason to say he is less.

The heretic in Colosse and his associates were guilty of such treason. They were giving Christ a place, but it was not the supreme place. Clinton E. Arnold offers this assessment of what was going on in Colosse:

> *People in the Lycus Valley fear the influence of astral powers, terrestrial spirits, and underworld powers that raise problems for them in day-to-day life. This fear did not instantly go away for the Colossian believers after they turned to Christ. They know the reality of these powers and must still deal with them. The question for them is: What difference does Christ make? For the ringleader of the new teaching at Colosse, Christ is functionally no more powerful than the angels they invoke for protection. For Paul, Christ is the exalted Lord, Creator of the universe, preeminent in everything, and infinitely superior to any kind of angelic power.[2]*

In the verses before us Paul demolishes this deficient view of Christ by stacking one truth about him upon another. As we examine his words, we find seven mighty assertions about Christ which can be placed under three headings.

Christ and God (v. 15)

Christ is the image of the invisible God

God is 'invisible.' He cannot be seen by the human eye, and he cannot be understood by the unaided human mind. But Jesus of Nazareth – and Jesus alone! – is 'the image' of this invisible God. This is the first of Paul's seven assertions.

We cannot get the full force of what the apostle was saying if we do not understand that the ancients regarded an image as more than a copy of some object. In their thinking, the copy of something participated in the substance of that object. The Theological Dictionary of the New Testament says of an image: 'It has a share in the reality. Indeed, it is the reality.'3

Paul's readers would have immediately understood what Paul was saying with the word 'image'. Jesus Christ was fully God. In saying this Paul was declaring that which the author of Hebrews says, namely, Christ is 'the brightness' of God's glory and 'the express image of His person' (Heb. 1:3).

When asked by Philip to show the Father to him and the other disciples, the Lord Jesus himself responded: 'Have I been with you so long, and yet you have not known Me, Philip? He who has seen Me has seen the Father; so how can you say, "Show us the Father"?' (John 14:9).

Jesus Christ perfectly and fully reflects and reveals God. The reason he does this is because he himself is God. The apostle John declares: 'No one has seen God at any time. The only begotten Son who is in the bosom of the Father, He has declared Him' (John 1:18).

Christ is the firstborn over all creation

When we hear the word 'firstborn', we immediately think in terms of time, but the term had another meaning in ancient times. The firstborn enjoyed special privileges and rank. This is the way in which Paul was using the word. He was not suggesting that Christ was the first person to be born. That would dismantle everything for which he was arguing. Christ could not have been the firstborn in this sense and have been God because God is eternal.

Paul was rather affirming that Christ has precedence in rank. He was essentially saying this: 'If you put Christ alongside any created being, he, the uncreated, has to be acknowledged as supreme in authority and dignity.'

The mood of the age is against claims of religious certainty. The idea of absolute truth is disdained and scorned. The pressure to diminish Christ is constant and unrelenting. We wilt under that pressure when we speak about God and say nothing about Christ, or when we 're-package' the Lord Jesus in such a way that he becomes acceptable to the modern age. Christians in general and pastors in particular must realize that they are not entitled to negotiate on the subject of Christ and still call him 'Lord'.

While holding steadfastly to the preeminence and the finality of Christ is absolutely essential, it is not enough. We must become so intoxicated with the Christ of the Bible that we are 'lost in wonder, love and praise'. It is not enough to hold the truth about Christ. We must love the Christ whose truth we hold.

Christ and creation (vv. 16-17)

Christ himself is the Creator (v. 16)

Instead of being created, Christ himself was the Creator. The Apostle John writes of Christ: 'All things were made through Him, and without Him nothing was made that was made' (John 1:3).

Paul could not be satisfied to only affirm that Christ is the creator of all. He wants to make sure his readers understand all that is included in this assertion: 'all things … that are in heaven and that are on earth, visible and invisible'.

He seems to be saying: 'Do you understand the magnitude of what I am saying? Go to heaven itself and look around. Christ made everything there. Come back now to earth. Christ made it all. He made everything that you can see, but he also made everything that you cannot see.'

All of that should have been enough, but Paul knew it was necessary to go even further. The Colossian heretics were very infatuated with angels, even to the point of putting them above Christ. To drive a stake in the heart of this error, Paul refers to 'thrones', 'dominions', 'principalities', and 'powers' (v. 16).

These all refer to various angelic orders, and Paul says Christ made them all. His point is clear — if Christ made them, he has to be superior to them.

The apostle is still not through. He adds: 'All things were created through Him and for Him.' In addition to being the Creator, the Lord Jesus was also the point of reference for creation. It was with a view to him that all things were created. He is the point or goal to which all creation is moving. We find that point powerfully stated by Paul in his letter to the Philippians 2:9-11. There he says of Christ: 'Therefore God has highly exalted Him and given Him the name which is above every name, that at the name of Jesus every knee should bow, of those in heaven, and of those on earth, and of those under the earth, and that every tongue should confess that Jesus Christ is Lord to the glory of God the Father.'

We need not understand all the details of Christ's creative work to understand the main point – Christ is indeed Lord of all. He is supreme. He must bow before no one, but all must bow before him.

Christ is before all things (v. 17)

To create all things, Christ had to exist 'before all things'. If he is before all things, he must be above all things. Therefore, he could not possibly occupy the lesser place given him by the heretical teaching that was being put forth in Colosse.

Christ holds all things together (v. 17)

The word 'consist' suggests continuation and control. The Lord who created the universe sustains it. He keeps it running. He is not to be compared, then, to the clockmaker who winds the clock and leaves it to run down. He is continually involved in his creation. He has not abandoned it.

Furthermore, he is actively at work in human history. William Hendriksen summarizes this truth in these words: 'It is the Son of God's love who holds in his almighty hands the reins of the universe and never even for one moment lets them slip out of his grasp'.[4]

Having come to the end of Paul's emphasis on Christ's relationship to creation, we do well to reflect for a moment. With astonishing brevity the apostle has covered stunning and exhilarating truths. Charles Erdman wraps it up in this way: 'This view of nature and of the whole realm of being, as created and controlled by Christ, is arresting and majestic. To see Christ as "existent behind all laws," to regard stars and atoms, and the worlds of men and of angels, as "in him" and "through him" and "unto him," is to gain a wholly new and overwhelming vision of his glory and to find a new beauty and splendour in the universe he has made and ever sustains.'[5]

The following resolutions will help us appreciate more fully the creating Christ:

> • I will each day seek to connect with creation. I will slow down and really look at the world around me, remembering that the book of Job tells us to 'stand still and consider' the created order (37:14) and the book of Psalms tells us that the various aspects of creation are to be 'Studied by all who have pleasure in them' (111:2). Therefore, I will seek each day to really look at birds, flowers, trees and clouds.

• I will connect creation with the triune God, remembering that all created things are 'the wondrous works of God' (Job 37:14) and 'The works of the Lord' (Ps. 111:2). I will look beyond the gifts to the Giver and will allow myself to marvel at his goodness, wisdom and power in providing it all. As I reflect on these things, I will remember to frequently sing:

> *This is my Father's world, and to my list'ning ears,*
> *All nature sings, and round me rings*
> *The music of the spheres.*
> *This is my Father's world, I rest me in the thought*
> *Of rocks and trees of skies and seas;*
> *His hands the wonders wrought.*
>
> *This is my Father's world, the birds their carols raise;*
> *The morning light, the lily white declare their Maker's praise.*
> *This is my Father's world, He shines in all that's fair;*
> *In the rustling grass I hear Him pass,*
> *He speaks to me ev'rywhere.*
>
> (Maltbie D. Babcock)

• I will connect the creative power and wisdom of God with myself, remembering that I can trust him to be sufficient for me in every circumstance of life (Matt. 6:25-34).

• I will connect this creation with the new creation. As I look around me, I will remember that this world, wonderful as it is, has been horribly marred by sin, and I will rejoice that God will eventually restore the natural order to its original beauty and glory (Rom. 8:19-21).

Christ and the church (v. 18)

Christ is the head of the church

Having demonstrated the superiority of Christ over the natural order, the apostle Paul now moves to do the same in the spiritual order. He does so by first asserting that Christ is 'the head of the body'.

As the head is supreme over the body, so is Christ supreme over his body, the church.

The Colossians would have recoiled at the sight of someone with two heads. The body has many members, but only one head. They should have also recoiled at the system proposed by the false teachers in their midst, that system which made Christ one spiritual source among many.

The church is the body of Christ. It has many members, but there is only one head, and that is Christ. As its head he exercises authority over it.

The head is, of course, indispensable to the body. The body can function without an arm or leg, but it cannot function without the head. While angels have been assigned to minister in various ways to the church (Heb. 1:14), the church can exist without angels. She cannot exist without Christ, who is the source and sustainer of her life.

Christ is the firstborn from the dead

Paul further demonstrates the supremacy of Christ over the church by calling him 'the beginning, the firstborn from the dead'.

Both of these terms relate to Christ's resurrection. Christ is 'the beginning' of the resurrection for his people. This does not mean that he was the first to arise from the dead. Others preceded him (1 Kings 17:17-22; 2 Kings 4:32-35; 13:20-21; Matt.

9:23-25; Luke 7:11-15; John 11:43-44) in this sense. But these all arose to die again. Christ is the first to rise to unending life.

With the phrase 'firstborn from the dead,' Paul both reinforces the point he has just made and carries his readers farther. He reinforces because 'firstborn,' as noted in the comments on verse 15, carries the idea of first in rank. Out of all those who have been raised from the dead and those who will be, the Lord Jesus Christ is supreme because of the special nature of his resurrection. But the term 'firstborn' goes further because it implies that others will follow. Christ, then, is not only living, but is also the living guarantee that all his people will follow him into resurrection life. He is, as Paul writes to the Corinthians, 'the firstfruits of those who have fallen asleep' (1 Cor. 15:20).

In writing those words, Paul was only repeating the promise of the Lord Jesus himself: 'Because I live, you will live also' (John 14:19).

Christians have, then, 'a living hope through the resurrection of Jesus Christ from the dead' (1 Peter 1:3). This hope will be realised when the risen Lord returns 'with a shout, with the voice of an archangel, and with the trumpet of God'. On that glad day, Paul triumphantly says: 'And the dead in Christ will rise first' (1 Thess. 4:16).

Having added to Christ's supremacy in creation his supremacy in the church, Paul comes to the crowning touch: 'that in all things He may have the preeminence' (v. 18).

If we have followed the apostle's argument, we must feel compelled to breathe – perhaps shout! – an 'Amen!' to this grand conclusion. The argument has been relentless, dominated by the steady drumbeat of the term 'all things':

- all things were created by Christ (v. 16)
- all things were created through and for Christ (v. 16)
- Christ is before all things (v. 17)
- all things consist in Christ (v. 17)

Who, having followed the apostle through these 'all things', can resist the final instalment, namely, Christ's preeminence in all things? The preceding 'all things' demand the concluding 'all things'. If we refuse to grant the latter, it is because we have failed to grasp the former.

The apostle has chased the enemies of Christ into their fortresses of falsity and demolished the same with the truth. There was no place left to hide and still claim to be logical. We cannot help but wonder if the religious guru of Colosse read Paul's letter. It is very likely that he did. If so, how did he respond to Paul's devastating arguments?

We may be sure that Paul did not take his readers through these various details out of mere academic, theoretical interest. He did not write to fill their heads with theology but out of a practical, pastoral interest. He wanted his readers to know the truth about Christ so they could stand against all the Christ-dethroning teachings of their day and could give Christ first place in their worship and in their daily lives. This passage has come down to us so we can do the same.

Kent Hughes applies the preeminence of Christ by saying of him: 'He must have first-place in everything.

- First-place in our families.
- First-place in our marriages.
- First-place in our professions.
- First-place in our mission and ministry.
- First-place in matters of the intellect.
- First-place in time.
- First-place in love.
- First-place in conversation.
- First-place in pleasures.
- First-place in eating.
- First-place in play.
- First-place in athletics.

- First-place in what we watch.
- First-place in art.
- First-place in music.
- First-place in worship.

Let us give him first-place.'[6]

Hughes' inclusion of ministry in his list reminds all preachers that Christ is to be given preeminence in their sermons.

For your journal...

1. What effect has Paul's teaching about the Lord Jesus Christ had on you? What are some ways in which you can show a greater appreciation and love for Christ?

2. What can you do to more enjoy creation?

3. What do you conclude from Paul's teaching on Christ as the head of the church? What can churches do to reflect this teaching?

Colossians 1:19

For it pleased the Father that in Him all the fullness should dwell...

Day 7
The Fullness of Christ

- Begin by reading Colossians 1:19-23
- Pray about what you have read
- Make notes on what you think God is teaching you
- Read the following chapter
- Answer the questions in the 'For your journal' section

We live in days in which many seem to think that there is no such thing as false teaching in the area of religion. They regard all teachings as being of equal value and insist that no particular teaching can claim finality.

Those who hold such views think of themselves as being wonderfully enlightened, and they tend to look upon the apostle as being bigoted and narrow. Paul knew far more than the sophisticates of our time think. He knew that one cannot be imprecise about the Lord Jesus Christ. Nothing less than eternal happiness hinges on our understanding of Christ. A diminished Christ cannot save and if Christ cannot save there is no salvation at all.

With keen awareness of what was at stake, the apostle laboured diligently to show his readers the supremacy of Christ (vv. 15-18). In the verses before us, he continues that argument. He tells his readers that God the Father has determined certain things about Christ. The implication is quite clear. If God had determined certain things about Christ, the Colossians had better determine the same things or they would be at war with God.

The fullness of Christ's person (v. 19)

What has God determined about Christ? The first thing is that 'all the fullness should dwell' in him (v. 19).

The apostle is not saying that at some point in time God the Father decided to give deity to God the Son. That would mean that there was a time at which Christ was less than God, and Paul's whole argument is that Christ is God and always has been God.

The fullness to which Paul refers, then, has to be a different kind. Geoffrey Wilson concludes: 'Hence this fulness must be regarded as the fulness which belongs to Christ … made flesh for our salvation.'[1]

The false teachers in Colosse were regarding the earthly Jesus as less than God. Paul was insisting that the fullness of the Godhead resided in Jesus during his time on the earth. In coming to earth, Jesus did not lose any of his deity. He was nothing less than God in human flesh. Yes, he was fully human, but he was at the same time fully God. Fully God, fully man — the God-man!

When Paul wrote that God determined all the fullness should dwell in Christ, he was essentially saying the same thing as the apostle John who wrote of Christ: 'And the Word became flesh and dwelt among us, and we beheld His glory, the glory as of the only begotten of the Father, full of grace and truth' (John 1:14).

The deity of Jesus Christ was always present while he was in our humanity. The humanity, while real, did not make the deity go away, and the deity kept, as it were, shining through. This was powerfully illustrated on the Mount of Transfiguration. There Peter, James and John saw the heavenly glory of Christ. Charles Erdman sums it up in this way: 'It is as if the monarch had been walking in disguise; only occasionally beneath his humble garment has been revealed a glimpse of the purple and gold. Here, for an hour, the disguise is withdrawn and the King appears in his real majesty and in the regal splendor of his divine glory.'[2]

If God determined that all the fullness of deity should dwell in Jesus, we must be careful what we assert about Jesus. We must not say, for instance, that he was 'just another man'. We must not say, 'Jesus made mistakes just like other men.' We must rather bow before Christ as our sovereign Lord.

Max Anders writes: 'It's impossible to give Jesus Christ mild approval when you understand him. Jesus Christ can be ignored or adored, but you can't give him mild approval. Jesus is our Creator, our Redeemer, and our Judge. You can't be casual about that.'[3]

The fullness of Christ's reconciliation (v. 20)

This verse begins a section which ends with verse 23. This 'lovely little paragraph'[4] brings us to the lovely work of reconciliation.

The apostle himself defines reconciliation when he adds the phrase 'having made peace' (v. 20).

Two parties are at odds with each other. They were once good friends, but something has come between them to drive them apart, and now they are alienated and estranged. To say they are reconciled means that the issue over which they have been in conflict has been dealt with and removed, and now they are friends again.

The Apostle Paul indicates that God has been alienated from both his creation and his creatures. What caused this alienation? We find the explanation in Genesis 3. Although Adam and Eve were made in the image of God, they rebelled against God. We might say they broke their friendship with God and formed a friendship with Satan.

Their sin had far-reaching implications. It involved all their descendants and the whole natural order. Many think sin is a very light thing. It is far from it. It is such an enormous and powerful thing that it made all human beings the enemies of God and even alienated all creation from God.

Our sin amounts to nothing less than a declaration of war against God. It is our saying to God: 'We don't like how you made things and the way you govern things, and we are now going to run things the way we want.'

God could have left the human race in sin. He could have left the friendship with Satan — and all its damaging consequences — stand. But in grace and kindness, he embarked on the work of reconciliation, that work which would break the friendship of a multitude of sinners with Satan, restore those sinners to friendship with God and even release creation itself from the horrific effects of sin. The reconciling work of God calls us to adoring worship and faithful service. The thought of the sovereign, holy God desiring friendship with sinners is beyond our ability to comprehend.

How is this work of reconciliation accomplished? By what means is it achieved? Paul leaves no doubt. It is all through the atoning death of the Lord Jesus Christ on the cross. R.C. Lucas notes:

> The ancient world knew what it was to ask questions about the baffling problems of reconciliation. But without the truth of the gospel there was no possibility of an answer so comprehensive, unqualified and decisive, as Paul gives here. It is not from man but God that the initiative has come: it is not through numberless emissaries that the work has been done but "through him", the one Christ: the impossibility, as men saw it then, of reconciliation between heaven and earth has found its solution, not in some "other-worldly drama" (Lohse) but precisely at a certain place, and at a time well

remembered, where Christ had endured a bloody and painful death on a Roman cross.[5]

We must always remember that God is the one who makes peace between sinners and himself. We sometimes hear people refer to making their peace with God. This statement is acceptable if it refers to accepting God's terms of peace, that is, depending completely on the redeeming death of his Son on the cross. There is no other ground for peace with God. We cannot make peace by offering God our terms, but only by accepting his.

The apostle had a very practical purpose in mind in writing these words. It was not merely to give his readers information. It was rather so they could see the dangerous heresy that was threatening them and so they could give Christ priority in every aspect of their lives.

Paul essentially points the Colossians to Christ's incarnation and his crucifixion. He says to them: 'Look at Jesus there in the flesh. Do you realise that he was not an ordinary man but was God in human flesh? Look at him now on the cross. Do you understand that he died there to reconcile you to God? It was not an angel on that cross who died for your sins. It was none other than God himself in human flesh taking upon himself the penalty for your sin.'

Do we realise these truths? We need them as much as the Colossians of old. Ours is also a time in which Christ is being denigrated and angels are being elevated. Such views will become utterly foolish to us when we realise who it was that died on that cross and why he was there.

For your journal...

1. Write down some areas in which we like to have precision. Why do we resist that same precision in the area of our relationship with God?

2. The apostle John affirms that he and the other disciples 'beheld' the glory of God in Jesus (John 1:14). Go through John's gospel. What episodes does John record that reflect that glory?

3. Jot down all the verses can you find that speak about us being enemies of God by nature. Record all the references that use some form of the word 'reconcile'.

Colossians 1:21

And you, who once were alienated and enemies in your mind by wicked works, yet now He has reconciled...

Day 8
The Riches of Reconciliation

- *Begin by reading Colossians 1:19-22*
- *Pray about what you have read*
- *Make notes on what you think God is teaching you*
- *Read the following chapter*
- *Answer the questions in the 'For your journal' section*

Reconciliation, as we have noted, brings parties in conflict into a state of peace and harmony. Through the death of Jesus on the cross, God brings sinners into a state of reconciliation with himself.

The supreme blessing in life is reconciliation with God. The apostle wanted the Colossians to understand that this reconciliation is available only through Christ. If reconciliation is life's supreme blessing and Christ is the provider of it, he must be regarded as the supreme being.

In the verses before us, Paul develops this theme of reconciliation more fully.

The future reconciliation of 'all things' through Christ

The apostle points his readers towards this aspect of God's reconciling work in these words: 'For it pleased the Father ... by

Him to reconcile all things to Himself, by Him, whether things on earth or things in heaven' (vv. 19a,20a).

As noted above, all of creation has been affected by human sin, and God's redemptive purpose includes restoring creation to its original beauty and glory (Rom. 8:18-22).

But 'all things' must not be taken to mean that every single individual will finally be saved. To hold such a view, we must deny this same apostle's frequent references to eternal destruction (Rom. 9:22; Phil. 3:19; 2 Thess. 1:9) and the wrath of God upon sinners (Rom. 1:18; 2:5,8; Eph. 2:1; 5:6; 1 Thess. 1:10; 2:16; 5:9).

Furthermore, if Paul is here asserting universalism, we must explain why he so quickly abandons it when he later writes: 'Because of these things the wrath of God is coming upon the sons of disobedience' (3:6).

Let's give the man credit for being intelligent enough to not contradict himself within the space of a few lines.

If we are to attribute to Paul — as we must — the teaching of eternal destruction, we cannot at this point attribute to him the teaching of universal salvation. How, then, are we to understand 'all things' being reconciled to God? William Hendriksen provides this answer:

> *There is, of course, a difference in the* manner *in which various creatures submit to Christ's rule and are "reconciled to God." Those who are and remain evil, whether men or angels, submit ruefully, unwillingly. In their case,* peace, harmony, *is* imposed, not welcomed. *But not only are their evil designs constantly being over-ruled for good, but these evil beings themselves have been, in principle, stripped of their power (Col. 2:15). They are brought into subjection (I Cor. 15:24-28; cf. Eph. 1:21,22), and "the God of peace*

(!) will bruise Satan under your feet shortly" (Rom. 16:20).
The good angels, on the other hand, submit joyfully, eagerly.
So do also the redeemed among men.[1]

The reconciliation of 'all things' will be achieved 'through the blood of His cross', that is, the blood that Jesus shed on the cross. The created order is not as God created it because of sin. Before it can be reconciled to God, the sin that caused alienation has to be dealt with and removed. There is only one way for sin to be taken out of the way. Its penalty has to be paid. Only then can the justice of God be satisfied. And what is the penalty for sin? It is death in all its forms — physical, spiritual and eternal (Rom. 5:12; 6:16,21,23; 8:6,13).

Jesus died on the cross for the express purpose of paying that penalty. The blood he shed there means his life was poured out in death. On the cross, he experienced death in all its forms so that the justice of God against sin could be satisfied and sin be taken out of the way.

The present reconciliation of the Colossians through Christ (vv. 21-22)

The reconciliation of all creation lies in the future. The reconciling of sinners has already begun, and the Colossians themselves were proofs of it. The apostle says of them: 'And you, who once were alienated and enemies in your mind by wicked works, yet now He has reconciled'.

The word 'alienated' tells us that the Colossians were once in a state of estrangement from God. They did not know him and were not in fellowship with him, but were separated from him. The term 'enemies' tells us that they were both hostile and hateful toward God. This intensifies their situation. One can be separated from another without having animosity towards him. The Colossians had both the separation and the hatred.

The phrase 'in your mind' gives us the seat of the animosity. One has to accept the truth of God in order to be saved, welcoming it 'not as the word of men, but as it is in truth, the word of God' (1 Thess. 2:13). On the other hand, those who perish do not 'receive the love of the truth, that they might be saved' (2 Thess. 2:10).

Paul adds the finishing touch of his bleak description with the words 'by wicked works.' This tells us that the animosity expressed itself in wilful disobedience to the laws of God. Sin is refusing to conform to God's will and way. It is the creature thumbing his nose at the Creator and saying: 'I refuse to live as you require. I will live as I choose.'

The apostle's measured words do not belong to the Colossians alone. They constitute a ringing indictment of every single member of the human race. This conclusion is inescapable when we lay Paul's description of the Colossians alongside similar descriptions in his other letters (Rom. 3:10-23; Eph. 2:1-3; 4:17-18).

How was the reconciliation of the Colossians achieved? It was also through Christ. Specifically, Paul says it was 'in the body of His flesh through death'.

God can have no peace with or fellowship with sinners until the sin standing between himself and those sinners is taken out of the way.

As far as sinners themselves are concerned, sin is a fairly insignificant matter and easily dealt with. If sin is the sticking-point, then reconciliation is simply a matter of God looking the other way. We might say it is a matter of God ignoring sin or dispensing with it by saying: 'I forgive you.' Left to themselves, sinners will always think of sin as insignificant and of salvation as easy. When they hear anyone approaching the matter differently, they will always wonder what all the fuss is about.

The thing sinners insist on doing is looking at the matter from their perspective. The thing they cannot bring themselves to do is consider the matter from God's perspective. They cannot understand that God is the offended party in the matter of our relationship to him, and the question is not what it takes to satisfy us on the matter of our sin — we are quite quickly and easily satisfied! — but rather what it takes to satisfy God on the matter.

We can only see sin as God does if we understand that he is perfectly holy. This not only means that he is free from sin himself but also that he cannot be ambivalent towards sin. It forbids him to take the 'live and let live' approach. It rather requires him to pronounce and to carry out judgement upon sin. To do otherwise would amount to God compromising his holy character. It would be for him to un-God himself, and this he cannot do.

God has already honoured the demands of his holy character in that he has pronounced judgement upon sinners, namely, separation from himself in that state which Paul describes as 'everlasting destruction' (2 Thess. 1:9).

But the very same God whose holy character requires him to judge sin is also so gracious that he desires to reconcile sinners to himself. Here is the huge dilemma: how could God at one and the same time honour his justice by punishing sinners and honour his grace by reconciling sinners? How could he on one hand bring such sinners into a state of peace within himself and on the other hand carry out his sentence of eternal separation? The cross of Christ is the answer. It was God's way of visiting the sentence of eternal separation on sinners while simultaneously providing the way for those very sinners to be restored to peace with himself. There on the cross, God poured out on his Son, the Lord Jesus Christ, the wrath that we deserved for our sins. The Lord Jesus there experienced an eternity's worth of separation from God. That is the reason for his cry: 'My God, My God, why have You forsaken Me?' (Matt. 27:46).

Now here is the glory of it all: God only requires that the penalty for our sin be paid once, and if Jesus paid it for us, there is no penalty left for us to pay. And because Jesus paid for our sin, there is no issue remaining between us and God and we are, therefore, reconciled to God through the death of his Son.

Furthermore, in attributing the Colossians' reconciliation to 'the body of His flesh through death', the apostle Paul refuted, in the words of Geoffrey Wilson, 'those who taught that angelic intermediaries assisted in the work of reconciliation. In opposing this speculation Paul emphasizes the fact that it was by the putting to death of this body of flesh that reconciliation was achieved, and thereby excludes these spiritual powers from any part in the work of salvation.'[2]

The future completion of the Colossians' reconciliation

God designed his reconciling work with eager anticipation of an indescribably glorious time, that time in which his people will appear before him in glory. They will then be 'holy, and blameless, and irreproachable'.

With the word 'holy,' the apostle intended to convey that the Colossians (and all God's reconciled people) have been transferred from a state of alienation or separation from God to a state of separation to God and his service. This state begins in this life and culminates in eternal glory.

The term 'blameless' denotes the absence of any moral blemish, while 'irreproachable' refers to being blameless.

We find the joyous anticipation of Paul expressed in similar fashion by Jude:

Now to Him who is able
to keep you from stumbling,
And to present you faultless
Before the presence of His glory
with exceeding joy,
To God our Saviour,
Who alone is wise,
Be glory and majesty,
Dominion and power,
Both now and forever.
Amen.
(Jude 24-25)

For your journal...

1. Read Revelation 21 & 22 for a description of the state of believers when reconciliation is complete. What will that life be like?

2. Read Romans 3:10-23 and Ephesians 2:1-3; 4:17-18. What details do these passages give about the sinful condition that alienates us from God?

Colossians 1:23

... if indeed you continue in the faith, grounded and stead-fast, and are not moved away from the hope of the gospel which you heard ...

Day 9
The Proof of Reconciliation

- *Begin by reading Colossians 1:23*
- *Pray about what you have read*
- *Make notes on what you think God is teaching you*
- *Read the following chapter*
- *Answer the questions in the 'For your journal' section*

The Apostle Paul urges his readers to 'continue in the faith, grounded and steadfast, and are not moved away from the hope of the gospel'.

The term 'not moved away' can be translated 'not shifting'. We can say, therefore, that Paul was calling on them to be steadfast.

What if they did not heed Paul's warning? What if they moved away from the gospel? The apostle gives a sobering answer.

Proof of an unreconciled state

He first says abandoning the gospel would prove that they had never truly been reconciled to God.

We must follow Paul's sequence. In verse 21 he writes: 'And you, who once were alienated and enemies in your mind by wicked works, yet now He has reconciled'. In verse 23 he writes: '...if indeed you continue in the faith, grounded and steadfast'.

His meaning is plain. We can claim reconciliation with God only if we continue in the faith. Steadfastness is the mark of genuineness. Or we can put it in this way: continuance is the mark of reality

We have this teaching on no less authority than that of the Lord Jesus Christ himself. To certain people who claimed to believe in him, he said: 'If you abide in My word, you are My disciples indeed' (John 8:31).

This truth is also explicitly affirmed in other places. The author of Hebrews writes: 'For we have become partakers of Christ if we hold the beginning of our confidence to the end' (Heb. 3:14).

The apostle John stated the same truth in this way: 'They went out from us, but they were not of us; for if they had been of us, they would have continued with us; but they went out that they might be made manifest, that none of them were of us' (1 John 2:19).

Those who do not continue in the faith have not lost it because salvation can never be lost. The problem is rather that they never had it.

Paul's teaching about continuing in the faith urges us to seriously reflect. Are not many horribly deluded about their salvation? They walked a church aisle and professed faith in Christ, and on the basis of that they believe that they have been truly saved. But there is no present evidence in their lives. They have fallen away from church attendance. They think nothing at all about skipping the observance of the Lord's Supper. They do not read the Bible and pray. God is not in their thoughts.

These people often think that they are okay. They believe they are saved because they 'went forward'. But salvation is not a matter of the moving of the body. It is a matter of God changing the heart. And if the heart is truly changed, it will evidence itself in changed behaviour.

The truth that such people need so desperately to hear is this: present evidence more accurately reflects our spiritual condition than past experience. This means if we are not continuing in the faith, we have no reason to believe that we ever possessed it.

Let us make sure we do not misunderstand. Those who do not continue in the faith have not lost it. True salvation can never be lost. The problem is that they never had it.

Paul was alarmed that the Colossians were showing signs of abandoning Christ. Perhaps you are where the Colossians were at the time of Paul's writing. You once professed faith in Christ, but now you are moving away from him. Your interest in spiritual things is lessening. Your commitment to Christ and the church is shaky. Please understand the serious nature of your situation. Don't attribute it to some phase you are going through. Examine yourself. Have you truly turned to Christ? If you have, you will never be able to abandon him.

Forfeiture of hope

From that point Paul moves to a second, that is, abandoning faith means abandoning hope.

The gospel of Jesus Christ offers an unspeakably glorious and precious hope. It tells us that the believer in Jesus Christ will be raised from the dead when the Lord Jesus returns and that he, the believer, will live in eternal bliss and glory with the Lord.

But that hope is tied to faith in Christ. Give up the faith, and you must also give up the hope. Paul is making it clear that there is only one way of salvation, and that way is faith in Christ.

This teaching is very unpopular. Going to heaven is such a simple matter that it is almost impossible to miss out. If you are a fairly decent person in this life, you will make it!

Why do Christians believe Christ is the only way to heaven? Are they just trying to be bigoted and narrow? The short answer is this: Christians are by definition followers of Christ, and the Lord Jesus Christ proclaimed himself as the sole hope for eternal salvation. On the night before he was crucified, he said to his disciples: 'I am the way, the truth, and the life. No one comes to the Father except through Me' (John 14:6).

Turning away from indisputable evidence

Paul has yet another word about the matter of moving away from the Christian faith, namely, abandoning faith means turning away from indisputable evidence

Paul, knowing well the many evidences for the truth of the Christian faith, could have gone into great detail here, but he gives only two such evidences.

The universality of the proclamation of the gospel

He first says the gospel 'was preached to every creature under heaven' (v. 23).

It seems likely that this is his way of referring to the Day of Pentecost (Acts 2:1-11). The gospel on that day was heard by so many people from so many nations that it allowed Paul to say, with a bit of poetic flourish, that the gospel was heard by every creature.

We should not try to make this statement pass the test of a strict literalness. He was speaking in a way with which we are all familiar. When someone says, 'Everyone is going to the new restaurant,' we do not take him or her to be saying that every single person without exception has gone to the restaurant.

With the phrase 'every creature' Paul was saying that the gospel was preached to so many on the Day of Pentecost that it was as if the whole world heard it. That day featured signs and wonders. The Holy Spirit came upon the disciples of the Lord Jesus, and they were able to speak in languages they had never learned so that all those from the various nations heard the gospel in their own language. The events of this day constituted solid evidence for the truth of the Christian faith. The risen Christ promised that it would come (Acts 1:4-8). The fact that his promise was fulfilled indicates that he was indeed the risen Christ.

It is important to remember that the signs and wonders of Pentecost were witnessed by great numbers. If one of two tell us they have witnessed something spectacular, we might be inclined to doubt. But if five or six or a dozen say the same, we are more inclined to believe. The signs of Pentecost were observed by thousands. If the Colossians moved away from their profession of faith, they would have to find some way to explain Pentecost. It was an event of such a nature that it could not just be left hanging without an explanation.

The experience of Paul

Paul gives a second line of evidence for the Christian faith in these simple words: 'I, Paul' (v. 23).

The apostle is essentially saying this: 'Before you Colossians listen to the false teachers in your midst and turn your backs on the Christian faith, think about me and the change that took place in me.'

Paul himself served as evidence for the validity of Christianity. He had been a persecutor of Christians, and now he was the foremost proclaimer of Christianity. The change came about because the risen Lord encountered him on the road to Damascus (Acts 9:1-22).

Anyone who knew Paul before and after his Damascus Road experience could not doubt the reality of the Lord Jesus Christ.

While the Colossians did not know Paul personally, his experience was so well documented and so well known that they had to consider it as powerful evidence.

For your journal...

1. Write down the names of some Bible characters who abandoned Christ. If you need help, look in a Bible dictionary for an entry under the titles 'Apostasy' or 'Apostates.'

2. Read John 6:60-71. Why did many of Jesus' 'disciples' depart from him? How many stayed with him? What reason did Simon Peter give for them doing so?

Colossians 1:28

Him we preach, warning every man and teaching every man in all wisdom, that we may present every man perfect in Christ Jesus.

Day 10
Diligence in Ministry

- *Begin by reading Colossians 1:24-29*
- *Pray about what you have read*
- *Make notes on what you think God is teaching you*
- *Read the following chapter*
- *Answer the questions in the 'For your journal' section*

Under the pressure of false teaching, some of the Colossians were beginning to drift away from their faith in Christ. The Apostle Paul was deeply concerned. He wanted them to know that the Christian faith was real and true and that they must remain true to it.

To show them the truth of their faith, Paul used himself as an example. With the words 'I, Paul' (v. 23), he reminded them that he had once been a blasphemer and a persecutor of the faith, but now he was a minister of that faith. How could they explain such a change in him if the Christian faith was not genuine?

Having mentioned his conversion and call to the ministry, the apostle now elaborates on his ministry. He digresses, as it were, with a word of personal testimony. In offering this testimony, Paul refers to his diligence in ministry and in prayer.

A sufferer (v. 24)

These words convey both Paul's response to his suffering and the reasons for it. What was his response? He writes, 'I now rejoice'.

It is easy to talk about how we should rejoice in the midst of our sufferings. It is another thing to do it. Paul was doing it. He wrote to the Colossians from a prison, and yet he rejoiced. Alexander Maclaren writes of the apostle: 'This bird sings in a darkened cage.'[1]

How was Paul able to respond to his suffering in this way? He understood the reasons for it. He gives one of those reasons in these words: 'I … fill up in my flesh what is lacking in the afflictions of Christ'.

Was Paul suggesting that something was lacking in the redeeming death of Christ? Was he saying that Christ's death could only go so far in achieving redemption and that he, Paul, must now go the rest of the way? He would have found the very suggestion to be utterly repugnant. No one believed more firmly than he that the death of Christ was totally sufficient for salvation.

He was not referring to the cross of Christ at all when he used the phrase 'the afflictions of Christ.' The word 'afflictions' is never used in the New Testament in reference to what Christ suffered on the cross. One possibility is that the apostle was referring to the afflictions that Christ had appointed for him. Paul was, as it were, given a certain quota of afflictions to bear for Christ, and he was now in the process of meeting the quota (Acts 9:16).

Paul's words contain great comfort for every saint of God. We are all appointed certain afflictions and hardships in this life, and we must meet the quota assigned to us. The comfort comes in knowing no more afflictions will come our way than what Christ has appointed and in knowing those he has assigned are for his glory and our good.

Another possibility is that Paul was referring to that which was lacking in himself. In this case, his afflictions were causing changes in him that were making him more like Christ.

A steward of God (vv. 25-28)

Paul says he 'became a minister according to the stewardship of God' which had been given him (v. 25). The term 'stewardship' refers to holding something in trust for another and administering it according to his wishes. In Paul's time it was commonplace for the head of a household to designate one of his servants to be his steward. It was the responsibility of the steward to supervise the household and all the master possessed in accordance with the master's desires.

Paul says he had been appointed by the Lord to serve as a steward in the following respects:

• He was to 'fulfill the Word of God' (v. 25). He was to preach the gospel in full measure, to preach it in its full scope.

• He was to declare 'the mystery' which had been 'hidden' but was now revealed (vv. 26-27). The word 'mystery' refers to truth that cannot be discovered by the unaided human mind. It is truth that has to be revealed by God himself. William Hendriksen offers this definition: '...a mystery is a person or a truth that would have remained unknown had not God revealed him or it. Such a mystery is said to have been revealed in the fullest sense only then when its significance is translated into historical reality. The mystery of which the apostle is thinking here in Col. 1:26,27 had been hidden; that is for ages and generations ... it had not been historically realised. It was present to be sure, in the plan of God and also in prophecy, but not in actuality. Now, however, that is, in this present era which began with the incarnation, and even more specifically with the proclamation of the gospel to the Gentiles, it was made manifest to his saints, that is, to the entire church of this new dispensation, none excepted. It was there for all to see!'.[2]

Paul here states the mystery of which he had been made a steward. He puts it in this way: 'Christ in you, the hope of glory' (v. 27).

Through the ministry of Paul, God was making it plain that Gentiles could now have the confident expectation of entering into eternal glory through faith in Christ alone. This had most certainly been planned by God and announced throughout the Old Testament era, but it was now actually being accomplished. And what a shock it was to the Jews! R.C.H. Lenski notes: 'At one time Judaism was solid in the opinion that no Gentile could possibly be saved except by becoming a Jew ... It was not easy for the revelation of the mystery to penetrate, namely that "Christ in you," in any man's heart meant "the hope of the (eternal) glory."'[3]

This truth — that the Gentiles through faith in Christ would share equally in the family of God with Jews — is also developed by Paul in his letter to the Ephesians (Eph. 2:11-3:13). What a marvel it was that Christ would come among believing Gentiles, take up residence in their hearts and, as a result, give them the confident expectation that they would enter eternal glory right along with believing Jews!

We must not rush past this without enjoying it. What Paul says about the Colossians applies equally to all Christians today. Every child of God has Christ dwelling within. The fact we have Christ indwelling us guarantees that we will eventually be with him in heaven, and that heaven is too glorious for words. Should this not make us feel like bowing in worship?

• He, Paul, was also to declare Christ. 'Him we preach, warning every man and teaching every man in all wisdom', Paul says (v. 28).

The words 'Him we preach', in light of what Paul has established, can be classified as a vast understatement. If Christ alone is the basis for firm assurance of life in eternal glory, Paul — and all preachers of all ages — had better preach him!

Would to God that those words 'Him we preach' could become fastened in the mind of every man who professes to be a preacher! Preachers are to preach Christ! (2 Cor. 4:5). They are to be so gripped by Christ and so inflamed by love for Christ that we can say a hearty 'Amen!' to these words:

> *Thou, O Christ, art all I want,*
> *More than all in Thee I find.*

Why are preachers to be so filled with Christ? Paul has been answering that question all along (vv. 13-23), but the answer of the immediate context is that it is Christ who gives his people the hope of glory. That in and of itself is reason enough for giving him priority.

But the preaching of Christ is not an easy thing. It requires 'warning,' that is, pointing out the errors of those who reject Christ and where those errors will lead. Unbelievers need such a ministry. They can be very comfortable and secure in their rejection of Christ, readily reciting what they consider to be solid reasons:

• The teachings of Christianity are old and outmoded.

They are not sufficient for modern, sophisticated times.

• All religions have their own ideas and teachings. This is used to go in one of two directions: no religion is valid or all religions are equally valid.

• If one tries to live a fairly moral and decent life, he will be accepted by God.

• There are so many who claim to be Christians that do not live as Christians. There must not, then, be anything to Christianity.

It is not enough, however, to warn. The minister of Christ must also teach. He is to lay out in the clearest possible manner the doctrines of Christianity. The man of God is to be 'able to teach'. (1 Tim. 3:2). He is to adopt the strategy set forth by the prophet Isaiah:

Precept upon precept,
Line upon line, line upon line,
Here a little, there a little...
                    (Isa. 38:13)

All of this requires 'wisdom'. It requires a clear-sighted understanding of the Word of God and of the times. It also requires the nerve to use the Bible to understand the times instead of using the times to understand the Bible.

Paul's threefold use of the phrase 'every man' (v. 28) embodies both the element of universality as well as that of individuality. The former reminds us of the missionary mandate of the church to take the gospel into all the world (Matt. 28:19-20; Mark 16:15). If the gospel is the only way of salvation, as Paul insists, compassion for others demands that we take it everywhere.

The latter reminds us that the gospel must not be proclaimed only to congregations but also to individuals we encounter along the way. Each pastor would do well to also take it as a reminder to address his congregation in such a way that each individual feels as if he or she is being personally addressed.

Paul was, then, to be a steward of the truth of God. That truth is found in the Word of God and in the Christ of God, and it was truth for the Gentiles as well as the Jews. Paul also knew he was a steward of souls. His goal, through the preaching and teaching of God's truth, was to 'present every man perfect in Christ Jesus' (v. 28).

How solemn is this! The preacher has been called by God himself to so faithfully declare the truth of God that believers will be brought to spiritual maturity.

No understanding of the gospel minister is more essential for modern day church members than that of the steward. Some wonder why the pastor insists on preaching certain themes. They fail to understand that he is a steward, and the steward is not free to do as he pleases. He can only do what his master prescribes.

A labourer (v. 29)

The apostle writes: 'To this end I labor, striving, according to His working which works in me mightily' (v. 29).

'To this end' refers to the aim the apostle has stated in verse 28. The word 'labour' means 'wearisome toil' or 'toiling with great effort and exertion'. The word 'labourer' doesn't fully convey what Paul is saying in these words. The word 'striving' takes us to the realm of athletic endeavour. It translates a Greek word which means 'to agonize'. The work of the ministry was such that the faithful discharge of it required Paul to strenuously exert himself and to struggle with tremendous effort.

It would have been too much for Paul if he had no strength but his own, but the same Lord whose work required such effort was also at work in Paul to supply the strength for the effort (v. 29). No pastor can succeed in the Lord's work apart from the Lord working in the pastor!

> *In giving these three pictures of himself and his work to the Colossians, Paul was not seeking their congratulations, adulation or sympathy. He wrote as he did for the good of his readers. They needed to understand that their spiritual development was linked to the value they placed upon the ministry of the Word. They also needed to understand that they too shared in the ministry of the Word. All Christians are not called to serve Christ in the way that Paul was, but all Christians are called to suffer for Christ, to be faithful to the truth of the Word and to diligently and fervently toil for Christ. By portraying his ministry as he did, Paul was essentially calling his readers to share in it.*

For your journal...

1. Read 2 Corinthians 11:11-33. Write down each instance of suffering that Paul mentions.

2. Read 1 Corinthians 4:1-2. What quality does the apostle identify as being essential for the steward? Make a note of some things you can to encourage your pastor to be faithful in his calling.

3. Read 2 Timothy 2:1-6. Jot down the three pictures Paul uses to convey the work of the gospel ministry.

Colossians 2:1

For I want you to know what a great conflict I have for you and those in Laodicea, and for as many as have not seen my face in the flesh.

Day 11
Diligence in Intercession

- *Begin by reading Colossians 2:1-3*
- *Pray about what you have read*
- *Make notes on what you think God is teaching you*
- *Read the following chapter*
- *Answer the questions in the 'For your journal' section*

Paul was never very far from prayer. We have to look no further than this letter to see this. After greeting the church, he offered a prayer of thanksgiving for them (1:3-8). He immediately followed that with a prayer of intercession for the church (1:9-12). We find him at it again in the verses before us. Here he describes for his readers something of the intercession in which he had engaged on their behalf. Nothing is more important and more difficult in all the Christian life than intercessory prayer.

How very important prayer is! We cannot go very far in the Bible until we are reminded to pray. The Word of God will not let us forget this vital duty.

The Lord Jesus Christ was a man of prayer. He 'often withdrew' to pray (Luke 5:16). On at least one occasion, he 'continued all night in prayer' (Luke 6:12). If Jesus, the God-man, thought it important to pray, how much more should we!

The apostle also laboured in prayer. He is an example to every Christian in this area. We must first note —

The intensity of Paul's intercession (v. 1)

We must not think the apostle writes 'I want you to know' to call attention to himself or to impress the Colossians with his efforts in prayer. From the first word of this letter, he has kept in view his purpose, that is, to warn the Colossians about the dangerous heresy in their midst. The issue is far too important to be momentarily laid aside while he gratifies his ego. He wants them to know the intense nature of his praying for them so they will realise the seriousness of the problem. No progress can be made against error until those whom it threatens see the seriousness of it.

How seriously did Paul regard the false teaching in Colosse? He says it had caused him 'a great conflict' or 'great agony' in his praying. How many of us regard prayer as a vital and indispensable element in helping others fend off false doctrine?

Satan's forces never oppose us quite so much as they do when we pray and pray seriously. Why? These forces know far better than we about the power of prayer. Satan laughs at our promotions, but he trembles when we bow in true, heartfelt prayer that earnestly lays hold of God.

What a terrific indictment we have in the example of Paul! He would not allow himself to be defeated in prayer, but, as noted, laboured in it. The sad truth is many modern day Christians seem bent on taking the labour out of Christianity. They would rather be tourists instead of pilgrims and vacationers instead of labourers.

The largeness of Paul's heart (v. 1)

These words tell us that in addition to praying for the Colossians ('for you'), Paul was also praying for the believers 'in Laodicea', and for all those who had not seen his 'face in the flesh'. The latter phrase probably refers to other Christians in the same general area (the Lycus Valley) who had, like the Colossians, been converted through the ministry of Epaphras. It almost certainly included those in the third major city of that area, Hierapolis, who had come to faith. The proximity of Laodicea and Hierapolis to Colosse virtually guaranteed that the saints there would soon be facing the same heretical teachings.

Here, then, is the largeness of Paul's heart — he felt concern for believers everywhere and not just for those with whom he was acquainted or with whom he was closely associated. We can express this largeness in this way: wherever one could find a believer in Christ, there he could also find the heart of Paul.

How often we race through the words of Scripture without thinking about them! Here we learn that Paul had been praying diligently for people he did not personally know and had not even met. How this reproves us! When we do finally get around to prayer, we are inclined to think exclusively of ourselves and our needs.

May God forgive us if this is our mindset! Let us learn from Paul to have a heart for the kingdom of God and to give it priority in our prayers. Let us pray for the untold multitudes who have never heard the gospel. Let us pray for the missionaries who are spreading the gospel. Let us pray for the work of other churches. Let us pray for revival to sweep across the nations. Those who wonder what they can do for the Lord have part of the answer here. They can pray about such matters.

There is so very much for which to pray when we stop being so occupied and absorbed with ourselves.

The focus of Paul's petitions (vv. 2-3)

That is some prayer! Let's break it down a bit.

Encouragement

First, Paul prayed 'that their hearts may be encouraged'. Charles Erdman notes that the word 'encouraged' means 'not consoled merely, but strengthened'. He writes: 'The word here denotes "not relief but reinforcement."'[1]

The Colossians were face to face with very challenging and strength-sapping trials, the most obvious of which were false teachings. They needed to be strengthened and encouraged in their faith, and Paul prays that they would be.

God's people today need encouragement and strength. We live in times which are increasingly hostile to our faith. Are we praying for our fellow-saints to be encouraged?

Love

Secondly, Paul wanted their hearts to be 'knit together in love'. He knew what we seem so often not to know, namely, there is strength in unity, and nothing is sadder than to see Christians at odds with each other. We must not put such a premium on unity that we are willing to sell the truth to maintain it. Paul himself serves as an example at this point. He was not willing to let his fellowship with the apostle Peter cause him to overlook the latter's compromise on the truth (Gal. 2:11-16).

While we are not to maintain unity to the cost of truth, we are definitely to have unity around that truth. Some might be inclined to think that we can stress such unity too much. Anyone who thinks so should go to a church that is riddled with dissension. Ask the people there how important unity is.

One of the primary ingredients in unity is humility. We cannot be united if we are each filled with ourselves, our thoughts and our desires (Phil. 2:1-11).

Assurance

Paul also prayed that the Colossians would attain to all 'riches of the full assurance of understanding, to the knowledge of the mystery of God, both of the Father and of Christ'.

There seems to be a definite sequence in his words. We cannot function as we ought without assurance, and we cannot have assurance without understanding. What are we to understand? Paul's answer is 'the mystery of God, both of the Father and of Christ' (v. 2b).

Let us keep in mind that when Paul uses the word 'mystery,' he is not referring to something that is hidden but rather to something that has been revealed.

God has revealed the truth about himself. As we apply ourselves to learning the truth, we find assurance flooding over us. How many need this word! We are so inclined to look for assurance in our feelings. Let us learn to look for it in what the Word of God has to say about the saving work of God the Father and God the Son. Faith comes by hearing and hearing by the Word of God (Rom. 10:17).

Paul adds this brief word about the Lord Jesus Christ: 'in whom are hidden all the treasures of wisdom and knowledge' (v. 3).

The apostle is here using the false teachers' words – 'hidden,' 'treasures', 'wisdom', 'knowledge' — but he is not speaking their language. We could say he is using their vocabulary but not their dictionary. It seems likely that these teachers were using these words to deliver this message to the Colossians: 'If you want to enter into the secret treasures of God's wisdom and knowledge, you must accept the truths that he has revealed to us.'

Paul responds by saying: 'If you want to enter into these treasures, you must accept the truths that God has revealed in Christ.' Those truths are 'hidden,' that is, stored in Christ. He is the treasure chest. But those who find him find the truths. William Hendriksen applies this truth in these words: 'The Colossians need not, must not, look for any source of happiness or of holiness outside of Christ. Do false teachers boast about their wisdom and their knowledge? Or about that of the angels? Neither man nor angel nor any other creature has anything at all to offer which cannot be found in incomparably superior essence and in infinite degree in Christ.'[2]

A mere glance at Paul's petitions challenges us. He was praying about spiritual matters. We so often pray only for temporal matters. There is nothing wrong in including such matters in our praying. The Lord Jesus himself taught us to say: "Give us this day our daily bread." (Matt. 6:11). The wrong comes in praying only for the temporal things, in never rising above them to pray for the spiritual well-being of our brothers and sisters in Christ

All of this gives us much to think about. May God help us to do that thinking, and may the spirit of prayer be rekindled in each of us.

For your journal...

1. Record some ways in which you can improve your intercessory prayer life.

2. Think about the requests you usually make when you pray. Write down some new and larger petitions you can include in the future.

Colossians 1:18b

As you have therefore received Christ Jesus the Lord, so walk in Him, rooted and built up in Him and established in the faith, as you have been taught, abounding in it with thanksgiving' (Colossians 2:6-7).

Day 12
Wise Words for Pressured Believers

- *Begin by reading Colossians 2:4-10*
- *Pray about what you have read*
- *Make notes on what you think God is teaching you*
- *Read the following chapter*
- *Answer the questions in the 'For your journal' section*

The Colossian church was being threatened by a complex set of false teachings. In the verses before us, the apostle Paul begins to unravel and expose the various threads of this heresy.

Each aspect or component of this heresy was concerned to offer the Colossians 'fullness.' Each one essentially said: 'You have faith in Jesus. That is good. Now to really experience the higher life, you must go on to do such and such.' Each of the various features of this heresy can be characterised, then, as a 'Christ plus' teaching.

'Christ plus' teachings are still with us. Christians are often asked if they are experiencing fullness or victory in their lives. Aware of their many deficiencies, all Christians have to say that they are not where they ought to be. Quick as a flash comes the answer: 'The problem is that we have not gone to the next level, and to get to that level we must go beyond Christ.'

To hear these people tell it, Christ is important, but he is not sufficient.

The apostle Paul responds to such teachings with the ringing affirmation that Christ is supreme and sufficient and all 'Christ plus' teachings are mistaken and dangerous.

Paul cautions and commends his readers (vv. 4-5)

He urges his readers not to allow themselves to be deceived by 'persuasive words.' Such words are the stock in trade of false teachers. In his letter to the Romans, Paul warns about 'smooth words and flattering speech' (Rom. 16:18).

Based on the report he had received from Epaphras, Paul knew that the Colossians had not yet been carried away by false teachings. He commends them for this. He does so by visualizing himself as being there with them. In his mind's eye he sees them standing in 'good order' and with 'steadfastness.' The term 'good order' comes from the military world. So far the Colossians had stood shoulder to shoulder as a mighty army in battle array. They had been united in their faith. The word 'steadfastness' is also a military term meaning 'firmness'. The Colossians had to this point been showing a solid front to the false teachers.

Many seem to think that false teaching died out with the Colossians and there is nothing for us to fear at this point. No matter how far some stray from the historic Christian faith, there are always those who see no danger. They are ever ready to explain such deviations as nothing more than a slight difference of emphasis or mere semantics. But false teaching is still present and still powerful, and the words of the apostle John are still in effect: 'Beloved, do not believe every spirit, but test the spirits, whether they are of God; because many false prophets have gone out into the world' (1 John 4:1).

What would the apostle Paul say of us if he were able to observe our response to the false teachings of this day? Would he

say 'good order?' Would he say 'solid front?' Or would he bemoan
and lament our lack of order and our lack of firmness?

The fact that the Colossians had done well up to the time of
Paul's writing did not mean they would continue. Past success
does not guarantee future success. Paul could not, therefore, be
satisfied to commend them. He knew it was also necessary for
him to add even more words of caution.

> *How many today are easy prey for 'persuasive words!' Let
> someone come along who has a very entertaining style and
> gets lots of laughs, and many soak up every word, believ-
> ing all the while that this teacher must be of God. We have
> not yet learned that we are to be more concerned with what
> a teacher says than we are with how he or she says it! We
> are better off listening to someone lisp or stammer 'Jesus is
> Lord' than we are listening to someone deny that truth even
> if he brings the house down while doing it. Let us always
> remember that Eve fell into sin because Satan spoke to her
> with persuasive words* (Gen. 3:1-6).

Paul further cautions his readers (vv. 6-8)

About forsaking Christ (vv. 6-7)

Having warned his readers about the danger of being taken in by
persuasive words, Paul turns to give them a guiding principle. In
effect, he says: 'You were converted by receiving a certain message about Jesus Christ. Why would you now consider moving
away from the Christ who saved you to embrace the different
Christ offered by the false teachers? You received a certain kind
of Christ, now stay with him.'

We learned early in our study that the Colossians came to
the knowledge of Christ through the ministry of Epaphras (1:7).

What kind of Christ had Epaphras preached to the Colossians? There is no reason for uncertainty about this. Epaphras had himself been converted under the preaching of Paul. The Christ preached by Epaphras was the Christ preached by Paul. What kind of Christ did Paul preach? It is all here in a nutshell. Paul preached 'Christ Jesus the Lord.'

What a world of meaning we have in those words! The word 'Christ' means 'anointed one.' It takes us to the threefold office Jesus fulfilled: prophet, priest and king. As prophet, Jesus declared the truth of God. As priest, he offered himself as the sacrifice for the sins of his people. As king, he rules over his people.

'Jesus' is the human name of the Son of God. It means 'Saviour' (Matt. 1:21).

The word 'Lord' means 'exalted one.' The Jesus who came to be our prophet, priest and king is the sovereign ruler of the universe.

This is the Christ the Colossians had received. They had not received Christ as a mere step on the road to God, but as God himself. They had not received a Christ who was a mere man, but rather as the one who was both fully God and fully man.

They had received a certain kind of Christ. Now they were to 'walk in Him.' They were to reflect his nature in their conduct.

They had received a certain kind of Christ. Now they were to be so 'rooted' in him that they could not be uprooted by the false teachers. They were not to give up the Christ they had received. If he had saved them, he was sufficient for them.

They had received a certain kind of Christ. Now they were to be 'built' in him. They could not be built up in their faith by departing from the very Christ they had received. They were to be built up in their faith in the Christ whom they had received.

They had received a certain kind of Christ. They were now to be 'established' in this Christ. They were not to waver in their faith in this Christ, no matter how persuasive the false teachers might be.

And while they were clinging to the Christ whom they had received in conversion, they were to do so with an abounding sense of 'thanksgiving.' The Christ they had received had saved them from their sins and from the wrath of God. That was indeed cause for thanksgiving.

All of this has great meaning and value for us. It is common these days to see people forsaking the very Christ they profess to have received at conversion. At that time they claimed to believe that the Christ who was fully God took unto himself full humanity. They further claimed to believe that while in our humanity he perfectly declared the truth of God and became the sacrifice for their sins. They professed to believe that he arose from the grave and rules today as Lord over all. That is the Christ they professed to receive when they were saved, but now things are different. Teachers came along with persuasive words, and these people who affirmed one kind of Christ when they professed faith now believe in one that is quite different. They no longer say he was fully God and fully man, but that he was only a man. They no longer believe that he perfectly declared the truth of God, but that he was often mistaken in his words. They no longer say he made a perfect sacrifice for sinners but rather that he died only as a martyr.

Let us make sure that we do not follow in the path of such people. Let us hold to the end the faith we professed at conversion — faith in Jesus Christ the Lord.

About false philosophy (v. 8)

Paul begins this section with the word 'Beware'. There was danger ahead of the Colossians, and he wanted to alert them. Picture a man suddenly coming to a place where a bridge has been washed away, and nothing is left but a raging torrent. Seeing that darkness is gathering and knowing other travellers are following, this man runs back and begins to warn them. The Apostle

Paul is this man. He has seen the danger, and he is warning the Colossians.

Or we can use the figure that Paul himself employs. He pictures himself as a watchman on the wall of the city. Seeing an army rapidly approaching, he begins to sound the alarm: 'The enemy is coming. Fight with all your might. Don't allow yourself to be taken captive.' That is, in fact, what he means with the words 'lest anyone cheat you' (v. 8). Those words can also be translated: 'Don't be taken as a spoil of war.'

In those days, conquerors would parade their captives through the streets as tokens of their victory. And after the parade was over, a life of slavery would begin. If the Colossians were not on guard, they would be taken captive and enslaved by false teaching.

The word 'philosophy' means 'love of wisdom'. We may rest assured that Paul himself was a lover of wisdom. His response to this particular threat must not, therefore, be construed as a plea for ignorance. It is rather his response to a false philosophy. It was a response to a teaching that posed as philosophy but really amounted to nothing more than 'empty deceit.'

The false teaching with which Paul was concerned had three major characteristics.

According to tradition

It was 'according to the tradition of men'. It had been handed down from one generation to another.

This reminds us that error is as old as Satan himself. What purports to be the latest or the newest is really nothing more than Satan re-packaging his false teachings.

The fact that something is handed down from one generation to the next does not necessarily mean it is bad. There are good traditions, and there are bad. The good are not in conflict with the Word of God. The bad are.

According to 'the basic principles'

It was also 'according to the basic principles of the world'. This phrase can also be translated as 'the elemental spirits of the world'. The New Geneva Study Bible presents this explanation: 'The Greek word translated "basic principles" was used in this time period to refer to gods of stars and planets, and even to the physical elements (earth, wind, fire, and water) that were thought to control the destiny of men and women.'[1]

Popular opinion was wrong, as is so often the case. These so-called spirit beings did not control these physical entities and forces. But there definitely were spirit beings who inspired and controlled the false teachings making the rounds in Colosse. Clinton E. Arnold writes: 'The basic point of Paul's teaching here is that the dangerous teaching at Colosse has a demonic root. Although it is passed along as human tradition, it can be traced to the inspiration of demonic spirits.'[2]

Not according to Christ

Furthermore, it was 'not according to Christ'. These teachings had not been taught by Christ himself or by any of his apostles. Charles Erdman writes of such teachings: 'They took men away from Christ. They weakened faith in Christ. They stood in the way of Christ. This is condemnation enough for any system of teaching or for any proud philosophy.'[3]

> *We are now in a position to see how very important this passage is for us. Many professing Christians still look for guidance from horoscopes and other extra-biblical sources. Many even go so far as to speak of having their own angel to guide them. Without realising it, they have been taken as a spoil in our spiritual warfare against Satan. They have fallen into the trap of a 'Christ plus' religion.*

For your journal...

1. Put down any 'Christ-plus' teachings that you have encountered.

2. Read 2 Peter 2:1-22. Record some of the major characteristics of false teachers.

3. Look up the word 'beware' in a concordance. Of what dangers do these verses warn?

Colossians 2:9

For in Him dwells all the fullness of the God bodily...

Day 13
The Sufficiency of Christ

- *Begin by reading Colossians 2:9-10*
- *Pray about what you have read*
- *Make notes on what you think God is teaching you*
- *Read the following chapter*
- *Answer the questions in the 'For your journal' section*

At this point Paul essentially says to his readers: 'Are these teachers offering you some kind of fullness? Don't pay any attention to them. All the fullness you need dwells in Christ and Christ alone.'

Do we understand what he is saying? With the word 'bodily,' Paul is taking the Colossians to the incarnation of Christ. The false teachers may very well have been diminishing Christ in the flesh. They saw the Jesus of history, not as God in human flesh, but rather as one of a series of emanations from God or steps to God. Picture it in this way: here is a very wide chasm between God and man. Jesus, as far as the false teachers were concerned, was one step in the crossing of this chasm.

Such teaching was a dagger in the heart of Paul. It brought him tremendous pain because it minimised Christ. Paul affirmed that the Lord Jesus Christ did not cross part of the chasm between heaven and earth. He crossed the whole chasm. When he came to earth, he was nothing less than God in human flesh.

And he came in human flesh so that he could go to the cross. There on the cross he completely paid for the sins of his people. On the basis of that redeeming death, he carries his people, not part of the way to God, but all the way.

It was in Christ that the Colossians had fullness. This did not mean that they were now little gods who shared his deity. It rather means that in Christ they had the source of all the grace, wisdom and strength they needed for the living of this life. There was no need, therefore, for them to seek grace, wisdom and strength from any other being. Why go to some other being when Christ is 'the head of all principality and power?'

Some day this life will be over. When it is, we will find ourselves in the eternal realm and face to face with the Christ who is Lord over all. On that day, every knee will bow before him and every tongue will confess his Lordship. And on that day, those who were not satisfied with Christ in this life but chased after 'Christ-plus' teachings will see their folly. There in the blaze of his glory, they will be amazed that they could have ever been so blind. And those who went through life affirming the supremacy and sufficiency of Christ will regret that they did not better serve him and better proclaim his sufficiency. The challenge before us is to live now as we shall wish we had lived on that day.

Completeness in Christ (vv. 11-15)

These verses bring us to the very core of Paul's letter. They enable us to reconstruct to some degree the false teaching with which the Colossian believers were confronted. As noted in the introduction, this teaching or philosophy was apparently a strange blend of Judaism, paganism and early gnosticism.

• It gave a very high and significant place to angels who were the agents through whom the law of Moses was given (Acts 7:53; Gal. 3:19; Heb. 2:2). The angels were regarded as being in control of everything that passed between human beings and God. F.F. Bruce writes: 'Since they controlled the lines of communication between God and man, all revelation from God to man and all prayer and worship from man to God could reach its goal only through their mediation and by their permission. It was therefore thought wise to cultivate their good will and pay them such homage as they desired.'[1]

• Since the angels were the ones through whom the law of Moses was given, it was regarded as essential to obey that law. Bruce explains: '...the keeping of the law was regarded as a tribute of obedience to them, and the breaking of the law incurred their displeasure and brought the law-breaker into debt and bondage to them.'[2]

• Appeasing the angels and keeping the law was regarded as the road to a spiritual 'fullness'. Those who travelled it were in a special spiritual class.

Paul responds to this situation by emphasizing again the complete sufficiency of Christ. His point is that there was no need for the Colossians to be looking for something beyond Christ. All they needed was to be found in him. Although the Colossians had boundless treasures in Christ, they could end up eating out of garbage cans of the false teachers.

Circumcised through Christ (v. 11)

Paul emphasizes the sufficiency of Christ by using the phrases 'in Him' (vv. 9,11) and 'with Him' (vv. 12-13).

The false teachers in Colosse were promoting the rite of circumcision. This operation, which consisted of the cutting away of the flesh on the male reproductive organ, was performed on every Jewish boy on his eighth day (Gen. 17:9-14; Lev. 12:3). The rite of circumcision was instituted by God to both initiate and signify membership in the covenant community.

Circumcision served as a perpetual reminder in the flesh of what had to take place in the spirit. It was an outward sign of an inward necessity. John MacArthur puts it this way: 'The cutting away of the male foreskin on the reproductive organ was a graphic way to demonstrate that man needed cleansing at the deepest level of his being. No other part of the human anatomy so demonstrates that depth of sin, inasmuch as that is the part of man that produces life—and all that he produces is sinful ... From the beginning, circumcision was used symbolically to illustrate the desperate need man had for cleansing of the heart.'[3]

After citing Scriptural evidence (Deut. 10:16; 30:6; Jer. 4:4; 9:26), MacArthur concludes: 'God was always concerned with the heart, not with the physical rite.'[4]

The thing that so many Israelites failed to see — and the thing which so many modern believers fail to see — is that God's covenant with Israel was never with mere Israelites. It was always with believing Israelites (Rom. 2:25,28; 9:6), that is, with those who repented of their sins and looked forward in faith to the coming of the Messiah. That failure soon led the people of Israel to regard the physical aspect of circumcision as the only requirement to enter the covenant community. They began to ignore the spiritual aspect it was intended to signify. That which God in goodness gives, men in sin soon distort.

The false teachers of Colosse may very well have been distorting circumcision even more by seeing it as a means to subjugate the flesh. The one who submitted to it would supposedly be able to move up to a higher spiritual plane. At the root of such teaching was the belief that the body is inherently evil. If the spirit is to soar, the body must be subjected and controlled through harsh treatment.

Paul emphatically declares that the circumcision required by the law of Moses is unnecessary. The reason is that Christians share in 'the circumcision made without hands', that is, one which is spiritual in nature. This is 'the circumcision of Christ'. Paul asserts, then, that when Christ died a type of circumcision took place, a circumcision which was so complete that it did not remove only a small portion of the body but put off 'the body of the sins of the flesh'.

The apostle was not saying, of course, that the Lord Jesus Christ had committed any sins and his crucifixion put those sins to an end. While Jesus committed no sins (2 Cor. 5:21; 1 John 3:5), he was in the body of the flesh (Rom. 8:3) which is the vehicle through which all the rest of us commit sins. When he died, he put off that body that is associated with sin. R.C. Sproul declares: '...the cross represented the supreme act of circumcision. When Jesus took the curse upon Himself, He so identified with our sin that He became a curse. God cut Him off and justly so. ... When Christ was hanging on the cross, the Father, as it were, turned His back on Christ. He removed His face. He turned out the lights. He cut off His Son. There was Jesus, the Son in whom the Father was well pleased. Now He hung in darkness, isolated from the Father, cut off from fellowship — fully receiving in Himself the curse of God — not for His own sin but for the sin He willingly bore by imputation for our sake.'[5]

Christians do not need circumcision for any spiritual purpose because they participated in Christ's death. When he died, they died. The circumcision he experienced on the cross applies, then, to all Christians. Joined with him, they also have put off 'the body of the sins of the flesh.' R.C.H. Lenski offers this explanation: '"The body of the flesh" is not the whole mass of sinful flesh, nor the whole physical body as composed of physical flesh, but the physical body as belonging to and dominated by sinful flesh. The Christian no longer has such a body."[6]

Here we are face to face with one of Paul's favourite doctrines, that is, union with Christ. It means that each believer was so joined with Christ in his living, dying and rising again that all that happened to Christ happened to them.

This is hard for us to understand, but the difficulty of it does not in any way lessen the truth of it. As a matter of fact, we are without exception always 'in' someone. When we come into this world, we are 'in' Adam. As the first man who ever lived, Adam was in a unique and extraordinary position. He was made the representative head of the entire human race. What Adam did counted for us all. If Adam had perfectly obeyed God, he would have secured eternal life and eternal glory for us all. But Adam sinned against God, and, in doing so, brought sin and all of its consequences upon all his descendants.

God could have left us in Adam. He was under no obligation to do anything at all about his sinful creatures, but he was unwilling to let sin have the final word. Even before the world began, the three persons of the Godhead entered into a covenant with each other. This was the covenant of redemption. This covenant required each of the three persons of the Trinity to perform certain tasks or roles. The Father chose for himself a people to redeem from sin. The Son agreed to pay the price for their redemption. And the Holy Spirit agreed to apply to their individual hearts the saving work of the Lord Jesus Christ.

We can look at this covenant in another way. We can say that the Father appointed the Son to be the head of another humanity, a humanity that would be redeemed from sin. When the Lord Jesus came, it was in the capacity of the second and last Adam. He was the second Adam in that there had not been another representative head after the first Adam. He was the last Adam in that there will never be another.

In the eternal councils of God, all who would believe in Christ were placed in Christ. They were in the mind of God so joined to Christ that what Christ did would count for them. It would be as if they had done it themselves. The law of God requires perfect obedience. We cannot render this obedience to God, but Jesus Christ did, and his obedience is reckoned as though it were ours.

The penalty for sin is eternal death, that is, eternal separation from God. When Jesus Christ went to the cross, he received that penalty in our place, and his receiving of it is reckoned by God to be ours. It is as if we died when Christ died.

When Jesus came out of the grave, believers came out with him. God looks upon them now as being free from the old life of sin and as living a new and heavenly life.

The marvel of all this inspired Paul to write: 'I have been crucified with Christ; it is no longer I who live but Christ lives in me; and the life which I now live in the flesh I live by faith in the Son of God, who loved me and gave Himself for me' (Gal. 2:20).

Here is the gist of it all: If Christ's death amounted to a circumcision and all Christians share in that death, all have been circumcised. There was, therefore, no need to submit to the false teachers at this point.

In The Holy War, *John Bunyan makes plain the Christian's struggle against sin. King Emmanuel has captured the city of Mansoul. He has defeated and driven out Satan who had been reigning there. The city is now under new management. But there are still pockets of determined and fierce resistance. Streets, houses and basements are still occupied by the enemy. These have to be located and put to the sword.*

Every Christian can identify with Bunyan's allegory. We know what it is to have pockets of resistance although we are under new ownership. The Christian's success in his struggle comes not from subjecting his body through harsh treatment, but from realizing who he is in Christ and living accordingly. When someone tells an adult to stop acting like a baby, we immediately understand. The person is being told to be what he is. He is an adult, and he is to conduct himself as an adult. No one ever tells a baby to stop acting like a baby. Because Christians have been circumcised in Christ, their duty is to live in a manner consistent with this truth.

For your journal...

1. Make a list of any indications you see that angels are being placed over the Lord Jesus Christ. Read Revelation 19:10 and 22:8-9. What did the angels in these verses say about the proper object of human worship?

2. Write down your thoughts about Paul's doctrine of the believer's complete union with Christ.

Colossians 2:13

And you, being dead in your trespasses and the uncircumcision of your flesh, He has made alive together with Him, having forgiven you all trespasses...

Day 14
Completeness in Christ

- *Begin by reading Colossians 2:12-15*
- *Pray about what you have read*
- *Make notes on what you think God is teaching you*
- *Read the following chapter*
- *Answer the questions in the 'For your journal' section*

The apostle is calling his readers to rejoice in the sufficiency of Christ. They did not need circumcision to raise them to a higher level of spirituality. They already possessed it in Jesus. Because of their union with Christ, they also had been buried, raised and made alive with Christ.

Buried and raised with Christ (v. 12)

Baptism is the means which God has appointed for Christians to signify their circumcision through Christ. When Christians are baptized they publicly declare their union with the death, burial and resurrection of Christ. F.F. Bruce says of early Christians who were baptized: 'They were, in fact, "buried" with Christ when they were plunged in the baptismal water, in token that they had died so far as their old life of sin was concerned; they were raised again with Christ when they emerged from the water, in token that they had received a new life, which was nothing less than participation in Christ's own resurrection life'.[1]

As important as baptism is, we must not regard it as contributing to salvation. To do so would be to repeat the mistake many of the Jews made with circumcision. Baptism symbolizes. It does not save. The spiritual death to sin and resurrection to life it represents come only 'through faith in the working of God'.

Salvation is ever the work of God. It is God doing for sinners what they cannot do for themselves. Even the faith by which they receive the saving work of Christ is a gift from God himself (Eph. 2:8-9).

Curtis R. Vaughn says: 'Baptism, then, is not a magic rite, but an act of obedience in which we confess our faith and symbolize the essence of our spiritual experience. Faith is the instrumental cause of that experience, and apart from real faith, baptism is an empty, meaningless ceremony.'[2]

By adding the phrase 'who raised Him from the dead', the apostle reminded his readers of the greatness of God's power that had worked in them. It was the same power that decisively and dramatically defeated death in the resurrection of Jesus. The fact that the resurrection of Jesus is attributed to the Father trumpets the truth that God was completely satisfied with the way in which Jesus carried out the work that he, the Father, had assigned to him — the glorious work of redemption.

The mighty power of God that accomplished the resurrection of Jesus gives Christians the confidence that they will also be raised from the dead. If God could do the former, there is no reason to think he cannot do the latter.

Faith is the only proper response to complete salvation through Christ. The puritan John Flavel observes of Christ: 'If he have finished the work what need of our additions? And if not, to what purpose are they? Can we finish that which Christ himself could not? But we would fain be shar-

ing with him in this honour, which he will never endure.
Did he finish the work by himself, and will he ever divide
the glory and praise of it with us? No, no, Christ is no half
Saviour. Oh it is an hard thing to bring these proud hearts
to live upon Christ for righteousness: we would fain add our
penny to make up Christ's sum. But if you would have it so
… you and your penny must perish together.[3]

Made alive with Christ (vv. 13-15)

The words 'And you' (v. 13) are emphatic. The apostle wants the
Colossians to appreciate the fact that the spiritual circumcision
provided by Christ had come to apply to them, even though they
were not Jews. It is as if he were saying: 'Imagine it! You Gentiles
have been brought into the wonderful saving works of God!'

He proceeds to remind them of their former condition. The
phrase 'being dead in your trespasses' suggests that their state of
spiritual deadness was evidenced by their trespasses, that is, their
violations of the laws of God. With the words 'the uncircumcision of your flesh,' he reminds them that their lack of physical
circumcision reflected their lack of spiritual circumcision, which
the physical was meant to symbolize. Paul uses the term as synonymous with paganism, which is itself synonymous with being
apart from God.

But the things that were once true of them are no longer.
Paul is able to triumphantly declare that they had been 'made
alive together with Him'. In other words, God had quickened
them through Christ.

How did God accomplish this? Paul answers with three major phrases, each of which begins with the word 'having'.

Having forgiven

The first is 'having forgiven you all trespasses' (v. 13).

This simple phrase contains worlds of meaning. The reality of human sin is here. The word 'trespasses' signifies 'a falling beside.' It suggests deviation from a path. God has laid out a path for each of us to follow. It is the path of righteousness. We trespass when we fail to follow it.

The enormity of God's grace is also here. The word 'forgiven' means those trespasses have been removed or sent away. They have been pardoned – 'all' of them. Partial forgiveness could only lead to partial relief of the burden of guilt. Total forgiveness leads to total relief.

The forgiveness comes, of course, from God. He is the one from whose path the Colossians had deviated. And it comes through the redeeming work of his Son, Jesus Christ (1:14). They could have excused their sins and forgiven themselves, but there could be no true forgiveness apart from God.

Their sins had rendered them spiritually dead in God's eyes. Therefore, they could not be made spiritually alive without their sins being dealt with. But God had dealt with them and removed them.

Having wiped out

The second phrase is: 'having wiped out the handwriting of requirements that was against us, which was contrary to us. And He has taken it out of the way, having nailed it to the cross' (v. 14).

With this phrase the apostle further explains the measures God took to grant spiritual life to the Colossians. The 'handwriting of requirements' is a reference to the law that God gave through Moses, the centrepiece of which is the moral law as expressed in the Ten Commandments.

This law is the standard by which all are to live. It sets forth the righteousness which God demands. This written law is 'against us,' that is, against the Colossians and Paul himself. It is, of course, safe to say that it is against all of us. It is so because it condemns us. Sin is failing to conform to the law of God, and we are all sinners by nature. This law, constantly pronouncing us dead in our sins, had to be taken out of the way in order for sinners to be granted spiritual life. We might say its voice had to be silenced. God could not make us alive as long as his own law was justly and continually pronouncing us spiritually dead.

The only way to silence the law — or, to use Paul's figure, cancel its handwriting — is to pay its penalty. That penalty must either be paid by the sinner himself or by someone who is willing to receive the penalty in place of the sinner. That person must, of course, have no sins of his own, in which case he would have to pay for his own and could not pay for those of anyone else.

The only person in all of human history who qualifies is the Lord Jesus Christ. On the cross, he received the full measurement of the wrath prescribed by the law, thus satisfying it. It is as if the Lord Jesus nailed the law to that very cross upon which he died, killing it as a condemning force against all those for whom he died. These are now free to obey Christ with hearts of gratitude.

How Paul loved to traverse the ground of salvation! He had been a great sinner — so much so that it might seem to the outside observer that he could not be forgiven. But human sin can never outweigh or outmeasure the grace of God. Paul had been forgiven! Now it was the joy and delight of his soul. We should not be surprised, therefore, to find Paul happily elbowing his way into this text — and carrying Timothy along with him! He does so by switching from the 'you' and 'your' which have dominated throughout to 'us'. He could keep his distance no longer. He must place himself in the joyful company of the redeemed.

Having disarmed

Paul has removed from the way to spiritual fullness both the rite of circumcision and every other requirement of the law of Moses. There was, however, one remaining issue, namely, the authority and power of the angels through whom the law was given. The false teachers called for reverence for these angels whom they supposed to be intermediaries between God and men.

We can picture these angels pronouncing as still being spiritually dead all those who ignored their mediation. Paul proceeds, then, to add yet another aspect of God's granting spiritual life to the Colossians, that is, Christ's complete defeat of all evil powers. These powers were in no position to pronounce the Colossians either spiritually dead or alive because Christ had decisively and irreversibly defeated them through his death on the cross. On that cross Jesus defeated the whole empire of evil. There he 'disarmed principalities and powers', making 'a public spectacle of them' and 'triumphing' over them.

On the cross, the Lord Jesus stripped the weapons from the hands of all demonic powers and made all of those powers his captives. As far as mere outward appearances were concerned, the cross looked as if it were a great defeat for Jesus. In reality, it was triumph for him and defeat for Satan. It was actually Jesus leading Satan and all the forces of hell in a victory parade. There is absolutely nothing, then, that they can use against the children of God. Geoffrey Wilson writes: 'As therefore only Christ is Lord, the good angels cannot lead the Colossians to God (1 Tim. 2.5), and the bad angels cannot separate them from God (Rom. 8.38.39).'[4]

F.F. Bruce adds: 'Christ crucified and risen is Lord of all; all the forces of the universe are subject to Him, not only the benign ones, but the hostile ones as well. They are all subject to Him as their Creator; the latter are subject to Him also as their Conqueror.'[5]

The apostle's words indicate that he regarded the teaching the Colossians were receiving about the importance of angels to be satanic in nature, of issuing from a demonic root. He calls the Colossians to understand the nature of the teaching they were getting and to understand that anyone who accepted it was embracing a defeated foe.

> *Paul attributes spiritual life to God. Some give the impression that sinners can bring spiritual life to themselves. They supposedly place their faith in the saving work of God through Christ, and God then rewards them for that faith by granting them spiritual life. But this is to put the cart before the horse. The spiritually dead are as incapable of spiritual action as the physically dead are of physical action. Those who are spiritually dead must first be made alive by God, and only then can they place faith in Christ. Salvation is, then, a matter of the grace of God.*

For your journal...

1. Jot down the things that stand out to you about your baptism.

2. Record your thoughts about Paul's three 'havings.'

Colossians 2:20-21

Therefore, if you died with Christ from the basic principles of the world, why, as though living in the world, do you subject yourselves to regulations — 'Do not touch, do not taste, do not handle'

Day 15
Therefore

- *Begin by reading Colossians 2:16-23*
- *Pray about what you have read*
- *Make notes on what you think God is teaching you*
- *Read the following chapter*
- *Answer the questions in the 'For your journal' section*

On the basis of what he has just established (vv. 11-15), the apostle comes to two exhortations, each signalled with the word 'therefore'. The first is that the Colossians should not allow others to subject them to needless requirements. Twice in this section he says 'Let no one' (vv. 16,18). The second is that they should not subject themselves to such requirements. They are, then, to watch others and to watch themselves.

Do not let others subject you (vv. 16-19)

The specific teachings about which Paul warned (vv. 16-17)

The teachings with which Paul was concerned at this particular point had to do with food, drink and sacred observances.

We must keep in mind that the teachers who had come to Colosse were offering a superior spirituality. The way for the

Colossians to attain this was, of course, to do what these teachers were suggesting.

R.C. Lucas helpfully divides the regulations of these false teachers into two parts. First, there were those things 'an authentic spirituality could not allow, and therefore must forbid'. And then there were 'those things which an authentic spirituality cannot do without ... and therefore must demand'.[1]

'Food' and 'drink' were among the things forbidden by these teachers. In other words, these teachers were promoting fasting as a means of securing higher spirituality. Geoffrey Wilson notes: '...in the ancient world it was believed that fasting made men receptive to ecstatic revelations from the gods.'[2]

The fact that Paul himself practised fasting (2 Cor. 11:27) means that he was not opposed to the practice per se. It rather suggests that he was opposed to the way in which the Colossian teachers were handling it, namely, making it a mandatory part of their scheme for higher living.

Among the things demanded by the false teachers were observances of 'festival or a new moon or sabbaths'.

Some Christians take Paul's warning to mean that it is wrong to observe Christmas and Easter. They even go so far as to say there is nothing special or sacred about the Lord's Day, and that we are free to treat it as any other day. But the fact that Paul has already referred to 'the basic principles of the world' (v. 8), the angelic beings and heavenly bodies which supposedly controlled people's lives, indicates that the Colossian heresy had a strong astrological element. It is likely, therefore, that Paul here had in mind the keeping of certain days to please the powers that direct the course of the stars and control the calendar.

R.C. Lucas thinks the teachers in Colosse 'had constructed a new religious calendar of fasts and feasts, based on Old Testament models, but "enriched" as they might claim by the best "insights" and treasures of paganism. Then the keeping of such a calendar, with its regular rhythm of festival, prayer and praise, may well have been mandatory for all who scale the spiritual heights.'[3]

The apostle's objection to such teachings is the same that he has offered throughout this second chapter, namely, that they shift the focus from where it properly belongs, that is, on the Lord Jesus Christ. As far as Paul was concerned, those who were making such rules and regulations the primary thing in their lives had moved away from Christ and were now living in the shadows (v. 17). The Christian does not need anything or anyone other than Christ and his redeeming work to experience fullness and victory. The apostle essentially says to these teachers: 'If you are still trying to "fill out" the spiritual experience of your hearers, you are living as if Christ had not yet come.'[4]

The teacher about whom Paul warned (vv. 18-19)

While there may very well have been several false teachers in Colosse, Paul's use of 'he' (v. 18) indicates that he had one in particular in mind. It is possible that this man was the dominant teacher after whom the others modelled themselves.

Paul begins his words of warning about this teacher with this plea: 'Let no one defraud you of your reward'. The word 'defraud' comes from a Greek word which is used to refer to an umpire or judge. Paul's point is clear. The Colossians are not to allow anyone to judge them or to pronounce an adverse decision against them in regard to their faith. In this context, the 'reward' may refer to that which Paul has been discussing at some length, that is, spiritual fullness. If this is the case, the apostle is essentially saying: 'Don't let this teacher and his associates tell you that you can have spiritual fullness only by following their agenda.'

Having delivered this word of warning, Paul proceeds to give four characteristics of the ringleader:

• He was 'taking delight in false humility.' Paul was in-
dicating that this teacher took pleasure in his practice
of fasting. This made him feel as if he were very humble.
How very easy it is for us to feel proud of ourselves for
doing religious things! This is the reason the Lord Jesus
taught us to not let our left hand know what our right
hand is doing (Matt. 6:3). We are not, in other words, to
congratulate ourselves for performing religious duties.

• He was taking delight in the 'worship of angels'. This
teacher and his fellow-teachers believed that God could
be reached and bad angels controlled through the influence of good angels.

• He was 'intruding into those things which he has not
seen' (New King James Version), is better translated 'taking his stand on visions he has seen' (New American
Standard Bible).

Here we are face to face with the hallmark of so much
false teaching, namely, its setting aside the Word of God
and appealing to visions and spiritual experiences. This
is a very old error. In Jeremiah's day, the Lord himself had
this to say about false prophets: 'I have heard what the
prophets have said who prophesy lies in My name, saying,
"I have dreamed, I have dreamed!" How long will this be
in the heart of the prophets who prophesy lies? Indeed
they are prophets of the deceit of their own heart, who
try to make My people forget My name by their dreams
which everyone tells his neighbor, as their fathers forgot
My name for Baal. "The prophet who has a dream, let
him tell a dream; and he who has My word, let him speak
My word faithfully. What is the chaff to the wheat?"' (Jer.
23:25-28).

Can words be clearer? The fact someone has seen a vision does not mean that he has heard from God or been sent by God. Our dreams and visions are uncertain ground, and when we set the sure Word of God aside to embrace them we are trading wheat for chaff.

• He was 'vainly puffed up by his fleshly mind.' This phrase, to quote R.C. Lucas again, '...describes the self-important person who claims to be full of inside knowledge on spiritual matters but who is, in fact, full of wind, or as we say colloquially, hot air.'[5]

• He was 'not holding fast to the Head.' The apostle continues his stinging indictment with the blunt assertion that the ringleader of the false teachers did not have a real and vital connection with the Lord Jesus Christ, who is the head of the church (Eph. 4:15).

One cannot deny the supremacy of Christ and still profess to have the good of the church at heart because Christ is as indispensable to the church as the head is to the body. From him 'all the body' is 'nourished and knit together by joints and ligaments'. Christ is the source and sustainer of the church's life. She is totally dependent upon him. The false teacher was probably encouraging an elitism in the church through private visions and experiences. Paul was emphasizing the oneness of the body in Christ.

The apostle also affirms that the church 'grows with the increase which is from God'. The false teacher was promising growth for the church through his Christ-minimizing agenda. Paul wanted the Colossians to understand that there is no true spiritual growth for the church apart from Christ. He is the means through which God supplies increase for the church.

Out of 2,293 passengers, 1,200 lost their lives when the Titanic went down in 1912. The disaster resulted in many changes which has saved many lives. Eternity itself will reveal how many have been saved from false teachings by Paul's warnings to the Colossians.

We must not think that he wrote these warnings because he was a difficult person who was jealous of the success of others. The severity of his warnings did not flow from the desire to be harsh and unloving but rather from the desire to see Christ glorified. Paul's objection to these teachings and those who taught them was the same as it had been all along, that is, they diminished the Christ who is the head of the church and from whom the church receives everything that she needs (v. 19).

Do not subject yourselves (vv. 20-23)

Paul now comes to his second 'therefore'. We should note at this point that the word 'if' does not suggest any doubt. It would be better translated 'since'. Paul is not raising a question but is again asserting the union of believers with Christ in his death. When a person dies, his relationship with others is ended. Christ died to fulfil the demands of the law and to defeat demonic powers. Since believers died with Christ, their relationship with those things is severed. They died out of those relationships. They should not go back to such things because those things no longer had any validity for them or hold over them.

Specifically, they had died with Christ 'from the basic principles of the world,' or 'the elemental spirits of the world'. As we have noted, the false teachers were claiming that the road to spiritual fullness included gaining victory over evil angels and spirits who controlled every detail of life. The way to do this, according to the false teachers, was to appeal to good angels. Paul reminds them again that the death of Christ had already secured the victory.

Paul characterizes the regulations to which Christians died in this graphic way: 'Do not touch, do not taste, do not handle'. The teachers in Colosse were suggesting that the very essence of spirituality was in avoiding certain things (primarily various kinds of food). Paul dismisses this teaching on the following grounds:

- Foods are perishable. They cease to exist after being digested and cannot, therefore, have any significance or value as far as eternal things are concerned (v. 21).

- Rules and regulations about such matters are human in their origin. They have been devised by men without the sanction of divine revelation (v. 21).

- Those who follow these humanly-devised regulations feel that they are being very wise (v. 23). While they think they are being very humble, it is a source of pride to them that they have imposed upon their bodies certain disciplines that others do not have the will to take up. While they are depriving their bodies of various things, they are in fact indulging their desire to be known as highly advanced in spiritual things.

The apostle Paul has covered a lot of ground in the space of the few verses we have examined. These verses offer many challenges and difficulties for those who try to interpret them. While we undoubtedly come away from them with the realisation that we have failed to understand every nuance, we need not be in doubt or suspense about their main teaching. Christianity is Christ. If we want spiritual fullness, it is to be found, not by looking away from Christ to other things, but looking more intently upon him and his redeeming death on the cross. Our victory does not come from seeking a second level of spirituality but rather from resting more fully and firmly on the level of the cross.

> *None other Lamb, none other Name,*
> *None other Hope in heaven or earth or sea,*
> *None other Hiding-place from guilt and shame,*
> *None beside Thee.*[6]
>
> (Christina Rossetti)

For your journal...

1. Read Jeremiah 23:16-32. Write a brief summary of what the Lord says about false prophets in these verses.

2. Read Isaiah 8:19-20; Acts 17:10-11. How are we to determine whether the teaching we are hearing is truly from God?

3. Write down any activities on which the Bible does not pronounce that have been forbidden or demanded in the interest of achieving a higher level of spirituality.

Colossians 3:1

If then you were raised with Christ, seek those things which are above, where Christ is sitting at the right hand of God...

Day 16
Looking to Things Above

- *Begin by reading Colossians 3:1-4*
- *Pray about what you have read*
- *Make notes on what you think God is teaching you*
- *Read the following chapter*
- *Answer the questions in the 'For your journal' section*

With these verses the apostle Paul moves from the negative to the positive. He lays aside, as it were, the armour of the soldier and dons the garb of the teacher. Here the noise of battle gives way to peaceful calm as the apostle lays before his readers their responsibilities as believers in Christ. The tone from 3:1 to 4:6 is that of 'sustained exhortation.'[1]

While it is obvious that Paul has moved away from the false teachers and their doctrines, we must not conclude that these exhortations have no connection at all with what he has said to this point. The sturdier the Colossians were in their practice of Christianity, the more likely they would be to stand firm against the alluring call of these teachers.

The apostle's exhortations in these verses can be gathered under two headings: looking to things above and dealing with things below. But Paul, master teacher that he was, could not be content to give exhortations alone. He sprinkles incentives along the way, and, in doing so, lifts the exhortations from the level of duty to that of privilege.

The 'seeking' aspect (v. 1)

What are 'those things which are above'? They are the exact opposite of 'things on the earth' (v. 2).

We know about the things of the earth. They are those things that pertain to life in this world. The person who lives for the things of this earth is the one who is so completely occupied with the here and now that he gives no thought to the spiritual and eternal realm. The person who seeks things above is the one who is conscious of another world and who consciously and deliberately orders his life to reflect that reality. R.C. Lucas writes: 'The Christian is one constantly looking upwards ... and drawing close to the throne of grace.'[2]

The Christian is one who has been given life from above, that is, from God, and he now seeks to reflect that life as he lives this life.

What incentive does the apostle give for his readers to live in this way? Here is his answer: 'If then you were raised with Christ' (v. 1).

The 'if' does not suggest any question or uncertainty. The sentence should be read in this way: 'Since you were raised with Christ.' Paul confronts us again, then, with the reality of believers' union with Christ. Believers died with Christ (2:20) and rose with him as well. Jesus' resurrection meant that he had finished with this realm of sin and had entered upon a new kind of life (Rom. 6:10). Martyn Lloyd-Jones writes of Christ: 'There was once a time when Christ was in the realm of sin and death; but He is no longer there, ... He is no longer living in the realm of, and under the reign of sin and death. He was there for a while, but He is no longer there. He is now living in this other realm, in the realm of the power and the glory of God – and in that alone.'[3]

The union of his people with him means, then, that they are to consider themselves dead to sin and living a new life in a new realm (Rom. 6:11). They are now to reflect that new life by acting as citizens of that new realm. Geoffrey Wilson says believers are to live in 'a manner which befits those who belong to the supernatural realm.'[4]

F.F. Bruce adds: 'When Christ left the tomb ... , He was raised on high, and is now enthroned at God's right hand. What does this mean for you? It means that since you have shared in His resurrection, your interests are now centered in Him, in that place of highest honour to which God has exalted Him. You must therefore pursue those things which belong to the heavenly realm where He reigns; your mind, your attitude, your ambitions, your whole outlook must be characterized by your living bond with the ascended Christ. Is this not a reasonable conclusion?'[5]

The 'setting' aspect (vv. 2-4)

The apostle is not simply repeating his first exhortation ('seek those things which are above'). He is rather taking his readers a step further. In addition to living with a consciousness of eternity, they are to make spiritual truths objects of careful and sustained study. The more Christians know about heaven the better they are able to live on earth.

R.C. Lucas commends the informed mind in these words: 'Without it we can find ourselves at the mercy of what are normally unreliable signposts, such as a sense of peace, a spiritual compulsion or inward leading, or some visionary experience. Without it our frail ship may easily be blown off course by every new wind of doctrine. Without it we still think like a child in spiritual matters, being yet unskilled in the word of righteousness. We can begin to walk the way of safety and true Christian spirituality only when we set our minds with diligence on things above.'[6]

To this duty Paul attaches three powerful incentives. He re-iterates the union of believers with Christ in his death ('for you died' - v. 3). He then moves to the hiddenness of their lives with Christ ('your life is hidden with Christ in God' - v. 3).

This hiddenness suggests both the secrecy and security of that life. Its secrecy means it is a life that is not understood by unbelievers. Its security means it is a life that can never be lost or destroyed. John Gill explains this latter aspect with these words: '...spiritual life is with him, as the head, root and fountain of it, and so is safe, and can never be lost; because he the head lives, the members shall live also'.[7]

The third incentive Paul gives is their future appearance with Christ in glory (v. 4). This life that is now hidden will not remain that way. The Lord Jesus Christ will some day return from heaven to gather his own. They will then come to a full understanding of the glory of their redemption, and the people of the world will come to understand that there is something to the Christian faith.

> The Lord Jesus said: 'For what is a man profited if he gains the whole world, and loses his own soul? Or what will a man give in exchange for his soul?' (Matt. 16:26).
>
> We could not gain the world if we were to try. We could not keep it if we could gain it. If we could both gain it and keep it, we would not be satisfied with it. If we could gain it, keep it and be satisfied with it, it still would not compare to the life God offers. How utterly foolish it is, then, to set our minds and hearts upon the things of the world! Let us rather lay up treasure in heaven (Matt. 6:19-21) and seek first the kingdom of God (Matt. 6:33).

For your journal...

1. What practical steps can you take to seek 'those things which are above?'

2. Write down some characteristics of Christians that are not understood by unbelievers.

Colossians 3:5

Therefore put to death your members which are on the earth...

Day 17
Dealing with Things Below

- Begin by reading Colossians 3:5-11
- Pray about what you have read
- Make notes on what you think God is teaching you
- Read the following chapter
- Answer the questions in the 'For your journal' section

While believers think about things above, they must deal with things below. Paul further exhorts his readers in this way: 'put to death your members which are on the earth' (v. 5). A bit later he adds: 'But now you must also put off all these' (v. 8).

With these words the apostle takes his readers back to their pre-conversion days when they used the members of their bodies in various sins. That was a time when they wore the garments of sin. Paul is here calling them to understand that their former way of living is completely out of keeping with their new lives in Christ. They are to no longer employ the members of their bodies in sin, and they are not to go back and put on the garments of sin that they discarded at conversion. They are rather to live in a manner consistent with their new lives.

Paul is not about to leave his readers to wonder about his meaning. He immediately proceeds to identify the sins that the Colossians must avoid.

Sexual sins (vv. 5-7)

They were to no longer use their bodies for any of the following:

- 'fornication', which refers to any and all sexual involvement outside marriage

- 'uncleanness', which refers to impurity in thought, word or deed

- 'passion', which refers to unchecked or unrestrained desire

- 'evil desire', which refers to craving what is forbidden

The context requires that the last item in this list, 'covetousness' (v. 5), be taken in the narrow sense of being greedy for sexual immorality, or in the wide sense of being greedy for anything that is forbidden by God. In either case, covetousness is idolatry. It is putting something above God and giving to that thing the devotion and allegiance that belong to God alone.

In addition to the incentive running throughout this section and repeated again in verse 7, namely, the behaviour demanded by new life in Christ, Paul adds this powerful and disturbing word: 'Because of these things the wrath of God is coming upon the sons of disobedience' (v. 6).

He is not suggesting that any Christian who falls into such terrible sins will lose his salvation and become an object of the wrath of God. True Christians can and do fall into grievous sins. The greatest of Israel's kings, David, stands as a lasting reminder to this truth (2 Sam. 11:1-27). The apostle is referring rather to that which is on-going and habitual. The next verse makes this clear. The Colossians had once 'walked' and 'lived' in these sins

(v. 7). That was their pattern before they were saved, but things were different with them now. They had been changed by Christ, and any involvement in such sins would constitute a temporary lapse rather than a continuing state.

The person who professes faith in Christ and lives continually in sin only gives evidence that he has never truly come to Christ.

We cannot leave this point without noting that the apostle Paul does not hesitate to attribute wrath to God (v. 6). How could it be otherwise? If God is a perfect being, he must be holy, and if he is holy he must hate sin and must judge it.

Sins of the disposition (v. 8)

Having dealt with sexual sins, Paul here moves to this new category. These are also out of keeping with new life in Christ. The Colossians were to put the following off as they would filthy garments:

- 'anger', which is deep, smouldering resentment

- 'wrath', which means a violent explosion of anger

- 'malice', which refers to hatred that seeks to harm others

Sins of the tongue (vv. 8-11)

Paul continues his list of sins by naming three that have to do with speaking:

- 'blasphemy,' which is both using the name of God casually – without reverence – and speaking evil of him

• 'filthy language,' which indicates general foulness or rottenness in speech

• 'lying,' which is speaking falsehood with the intention of misleading. We may wonder why this sin is given special emphasis. Matthew Henry answers in this way: '...it is contrary both to the law of truth and the law of love, it is both unjust and unkind, and naturally tends to destroy all faith and friendship among mankind. Lying makes us like the devil (who is the father of lies), and is a prime part of the devil's image upon our souls'.[1]

As we ponder the vices listed by Paul, we cannot help but agree with Charles Erdman: 'It is glorious to be a Christian; it is not easy.'[2]

The apostle could not conclude this section without again reminding his readers of its dominating thought, namely, their new life in Christ. They have put off the old man (what they were in Adam) and they have put on the new man (what they are in Christ). They are now involved in the process of continually being renewed in their knowledge of Christ and growing into his image (vv. 9-10).

One of the primary features of life in Christ is the elimination of surface distinctions. The false teachers who were troubling the Colossians delighted in offering experiences and teachers that created an elite in the church. The gospel does just the opposite. Christianity removes distinctions between race ('Greek nor Jew'), religion ('circumcised nor uncircumcised'), culture ('barbarian, Scythian') and social standing ('slave nor free'). Regarding the barbarians and Scythians, John MacArthur writes: 'Strong cultural barriers also pervaded the ancient world. The cultured, educated Greek or Jew looked with contempt on the barbarian of Scythian. Barbarian was an onomotopoetic word used to describe people who spoke an inarticulate and stammering speech. The Greeks intended it as a term of derision on those who were not among the elite (i.e., themselves). The Scythians, above all barbarians, were hated and feared. They were a nomadic, warlike people who invaded the Fertile Crescent in the seventh century before Christ. The Scythians were notorious for their savagery. ... A fellowship including Greeks, Jews, and Scythians was unthinkable in the ancient world. Yet that is precisely what happened in the church. Christ demolished the cultural barriers separating men.'[3]

The gospel rather creates a marvellous unity in which 'Christ is all and in all' (v. 11).

> *Christianity is not a matter of tacking a few Christian activities on to our lives. It makes a fundamental and lasting change in the person himself. It affects, therefore, all of life. Because of this change, the Christian wants each aspect of his life to comply with the commandments of God. While the Christian will never be perfect in this life, he will also never be at peace with sin. No one who has enjoyed a refreshing bath or shower desires to dress in ragged, smelly clothes when clean clothes are readily available.*

For your journal...

1. Make a list of practical steps you can take to avoid sexual sins.

2. Jot down some steps you can take to guard against sins of the disposition.

3. Record some steps you can take to avoid sins of the tongue.

Colossians 3:14

But above all these things put on love, which is the bond of perfection.

Day 18
What to Put On

- *Begin by reading Colossians 3:12-14*
- *Pray about what you have read*
- *Make notes on what you think God is teaching you*
- *Read the following chapter*
- *Answer the questions in the 'For your journal' section*

The Apostle Paul continues to exhort his readers in these verses. Here, however, the tone is positive instead of negative. In other words, he shifts from what the Colossians are not to practice to those things which they are to practice. He moves from vices to virtues. He also seems to shift from the Christian's personal life to his church life and his relationship with his brothers and sisters in Christ .

Paul's exhortations in this section can be placed under three headings: 'put on', 'let' and 'do'. Today we consider only the 'put on' exhortation.

Why they were to do this (v. 12)

As we have noticed previously, the apostle Paul was a master of weaving delightful incentives into his presentations of Christian duty. He gives his readers a marvellous incentive before he mentions the first duty. He does so by calling them 'the elect of God, holy and beloved' (v. 12).

The phrase 'elect of God' means they were chosen by God. Their salvation ultimately had to be traced, not to their choice of God, but rather to his choice of them. In his letter to the Ephesians, the apostle Paul emphasized God's choice of his people with these words: 'He chose us in Him before the foundation of the world, that we should be holy and without blame before Him in love, having predestined us to adoption as sons by Jesus Christ to Himself, according to the good pleasure of His will, to the praise of the glory of His grace, by which He has made us accepted in the Beloved' (Eph. 1:4-6).

As a result of God's choice, the Colossians were 'holy and beloved'. The word 'holy' means 'set apart'. God chose his people for the express purpose of setting them apart to serve him. Furthermore, in choosing them God had set his love upon them, making them one with his 'Beloved,' namely, Christ. To be one with him means God's people are loved by God as certainly as Christ is.

These titles were not the exclusive property of believers in Colosse. They belong equally to the children of God of all ages. What a blessing it is to be a child of God!

What they were to do (vv. 13-14)

After reminding them of their election, Paul calls his readers to 'put on' eight graces. Geoffrey Wilson says of these graces: 'Since the church is a mixed community, the virtues listed by Paul all have to do with personal relationships, and are designed to promote peace and harmony amongst those who by background and temperament were once poles apart.'[1]

'tender mercies' (v. 12). This means, as some translate, to have 'a heart of compassion.' This is a heart is touched and grieved by the misery of others. This trait was perfectly expressed by the Lord Jesus. He was always moved at the sight of human need (Matt. 9:35-36).

'kindness' (v. 12). Charles Erdman defines kindness as ' … that goodness of heart which enables a man to meet the world with a smile and to act generously toward others, responding with cheerfulness to every call for help.'[2]

It is that trait which takes the sharp edge of harshness from us.

'humbleness of mind' (v. 12). This phrase can also be translated with the word 'lowliness.' It is that trait which causes one to not insist on his own rights but to seek the good of others. Its supreme expression is found again in the Lord Jesus Christ (Phil. 2:5-11).

'meekness' (v. 12). This is the spirit that refuses to grumble or take offense in the midst of difficult and trying circumstances.

'longsuffering' (v. 12). This is the ability to endure provocation without being ruffled or riled to anger.

'bearing with one another' (v. 13). This indicates that quality which enables one to lovingly put up with unpleasant traits in others.

'forgiving one another' (v. 13). This refers to freely and unconditionally bestowing pardon upon anyone who has wronged us.

The apostle attaches to this exhortation the powerful incentive of Christ who has freely forgiven all his people of their sins even though they did not deserve it. Christians cannot, therefore, withhold from others that which they have so graciously received.

The cross of Calvary takes away every hiding-place from those who refuse to forgive. If we refuse to forgive someone because he doesn't deserve it, we must look to the cross where Jesus died for us while we were ungodly and undeserving.

If we refuse to forgive because of the greatness of the offence perpetrated against us, we must look again to the cross. No greater offence could ever be committed than that which sinners have levelled against God. And yet God took our humanity, and in that humanity went to the cross, where Jesus cried: 'Father, forgive them' (Luke 23:34).

If we withhold forgiveness because we are waiting for the other person to take the first step, we must look to the cross which amounts to God covering the whole distance between himself and sinners who could not cover any distance at all.

The cross is ever the antidote for a sour disposition and an unforgiving spirit. If we persist in such things, we only give evidence that we have studied thoroughly and deeply its lessons.

'love' (v. 14). This is tender affection and devotion to another. Paul calls the Colossians to put on this grace 'above all' or 'on top of all' as the article that completes and pulls all the other articles together, which makes it 'the bond of perfection'.

We must not separate the duty to 'put on' Christian graces from who we are in Christ, 'the elect of God, holy and beloved.' Our identity in Christ provides our incentive for living the Christian life. To the degree that we more fully understand the incalculable 'reach' of salvation, we will be inclined to manifest its life-changing power. How great is that reach? It stretches from eternity to eternity. Every Christian was chosen in eternity past by the sovereign, gracious act of God, and that grace will finally and unfailingly carry each Christian into the glories of eternity to come. This fills the Christian with awe and makes him desire to live for the honour of such a God. The Christian does not look at his life through the lens of duty to begrudgingly say 'I must.' He rather looks at his duties through the lens of redeeming love, exclaims 'Such a God! Such grace!' and gladly says 'I will!'

For your journal...

1. In verse 12, the apostle calls his readers 'the elect of God.' Read Ephesians 1:3-5. Jot down the major points Paul makes in this passage about election.

2. Name some specific ways in which you can seek 'those things which are above?'

Colossians 3:15,16,17

Let the peace of God rule in your hearts ... Let the word of Christ dwell in your richly ... do all in the name of the Lord Jesus.

Day 19
Letting and Doing

- *Begin by reading Colossians 3:15-17*
- *Pray about what you have read*
- *Make notes on what you think God is teaching you*
- *Read the following chapter*
- *Answer the questions in the 'For your journal' section*

After urging the Colossians to 'put on' these eight graces, the apostle gives them two exhortations signalled by the word 'let' and another signalled by the word 'do' (v. 17).

'let' (vv. 15-16)

'Let the peace of God rule in your hearts'

Peace is one of the central words of the Christian faith. We are sinners by nature, and part of our sinful nature is lack of peace. The gospel of Christ produces peace. It puts us at peace with God, it brings us peace within and it puts us at peace with those around us.

In urging the Colossians to 'let the peace of God rule' in their hearts, the apostle was calling them to remember the peace-making nature of the gospel and to let that peace control and govern them. While others were being swept along by turbulent tides, the Colossians were to let peace be their umpire (such is the meaning of the Greek word which is translated 'rule'). The apostle, it seems, was picturing his readers as being torn by the pressures and questions of life. How were they to determine what they were to do? Paul indicates that they were to choose the course that tended toward peace, that is, that course which reflected the peace of God.

John Gill writes: '...the saints ... are called to peace by God, who is the God of peace; by Christ, who is the Prince of peace; and by the Spirit, whose fruit is peace; and through the Gospel, which is the Gospel of peace, and into a Gospel state, which lies in peace, righteousness, and joy in the Holy Ghost; and they not only called to this, but they are called in one body: though they are many members, yet they are but one body; and therefore ought to be in peace, and that should bear the sway in them, seeing it is unnatural for members of the same body to quarrel with each other.'[1]

Before he turns from the theme of peace, Paul urges his readers to 'be thankful' (v. 15). This is not a mere 'throw-in'. It is rather the inevitable result of peace. If we have peace in our hearts, it will come out our mouths. On the other hand, a complaining tongue is not fed by a peaceful heart.

'Let the Word of Christ dwell in you richly'

The apostle also urged the Colossians to 'let the Word of Christ dwell' in them in rich measure.

What is the 'Word of Christ?' It is the same as the Word of God which we have in the Scriptures. When we take the Bible in our hands, we are holding the words of Christ himself. What an awesome thought! What a priceless treasure we have in the Bible!

It is not enough, however, to hold the Bible in our hands. We must hold it in our hearts, and do so, not meagrely, but abundantly.

It is interesting to compare this portion of Paul's letter to Ephesians 5:18-21. It is immediately apparent that the passages are almost identical. One notable difference is that Paul tells the Ephesians to be Spirit-filled (Eph. 5:18) and the Colossians to be Word-filled. It should be obvious to us that he was not telling the Ephesians one thing and the Colossians something quite different. To be Spirit-filled is to be Word-filled, and to be Word-filled is to be Spirit-filled. Those who are most controlled by the Word of God are those who are most governed and controlled by the Spirit of God because, as Paul says to the Ephesians, '...the sword of the Spirit ... is the word of God' (Eph. 6:17).

The effect of a richly dwelling word is that God's people will be able to teach and admonish each other. The teaching refers to the imparting of the doctrines of the Christian faith. The admonishing has to do with the giving of practical instructions and warnings about how to live.

We associate such teaching and admonishing with the spoken word, but, while not denying that, the apostle connects it with singing.

As ruling peace comes out in thankful praise, so here a richly dwelling Word comes out in 'psalms and hymns and spiritual songs'. The psalms probably refer to the Psalms of the Old Testament. The hymns may refer to more formal songs of praise, while spiritual songs to those of a more impromptu nature. Curtis Vaughn is surely correct: 'The language is intended to emphasize rich variety of song, not to give instruction in ancient hymnody. Essentially the three terms are employed to heighten the idea of joyousness called for in the passage.'[2]

All Christian singing is to consist of three elements. It is to be with grace, from the heart and to God. Our singing is not, then, to be an empty formality in which we merely mouth words. It is to come from hearts that are conscious of having been touched by God's grace and are grateful for that touch. It is to be hearty and robust. It is be done with the consciousness that we are worshipping God and directly addressing him.

To let the Word of Christ dwell richly within, we must read it:

- *confidently*, knowing it is true and dependable (Ps. 119:142,151,160; 2 Tim. 3:16; 2 Peter 1:21)
- *joyfully* (Ps. 119:14,162)
- *diligently* (Acts 17:11; 2 Tim. 2:15)
- *reverently* (Ps. 119:161; Isa. 66:2,5)
- *Christ-centredly* (Luke 24:27,44-45; John 5:39; Acts 8:35; 2 Tim. 3:14-15)
- *experientially* (is there a promise for me to believe? a command for me to obey? an example for me to emulate?)

'do' (v. 17)

The apostle brings this part of his letter to a close by offering this exhortation: 'do all in the name of the Lord Jesus'.

When someone speaks my name, he or she is speaking about me. My name is not separate from me. It represents me, the person, and the name of Christ represents him. To do all in the name of Christ is, therefore, to do all in accordance with the nature of Christ and with awareness that we represent him.

This provides us with a 'rule of thumb' for living. In every situation the Christian can ask, in the words of F.F. Bruce, 'What is the Christian thing to do here? Can I do this without compromising my Christian confession? Can I do it … 'in the name of the Lord Jesus'? (For His reputation is at stake in the lives and conduct of His known followers).'[3]

Not wanting the Colossians to forget about the importance of being thankful, the apostle attaches it to this duty as well. As Christians go about the business of doing all in the name of Christ, they are to be grateful that they have been afforded the privilege of being Christ's people and can serve as his representatives.

The responsibility to do all in the name of the Lord Jesus is illustrated in an experience related in Jerry Bridges book I Will Give You Glory, O God:

> *My wife and I once stopped at a bakery with what we thought was a "two for the price of one" coupon. It's a small specialty bakery where a salesclerk waits on each customer. My wife selected two loaves of bread and handed the young lady our coupon. "I'm sorry," the clerk said," but this coupon is good only at the new store we just opened." The coupon didn't state this limitation, but that's what the bakery intended, and they stuck to it (not good customer relations in my opinion, but that's beside the point of the story). My wife said, "Well, just give me one loaf," and she paid for it. As the clerk entered the transaction in her cash register she said to us, "You people are so nice to me."*
>
> *"What do you mean," I asked.*
>
> *"People have been angry at me all day over this coupon deal," she replied, "and you didn't get angry."*
>
> *Later my wife and I talked about how we could have used that brief conversation as a means of witness, which we had failed to do. But the lesson I learned from that shopping event is this: As a Christian I am never "off duty." Even in*

such an ordinary event as buying a loaf of bread, I have an opportunity to either glorify God or shame Him by the way I conduct myself.[4]

Later Bridges adds these words:

Life is largely a mosaic of little things: routine events, everyday duties, and ordinary conversations. How we conduct ourselves in these circumstances determines to a great extent whether we glorify God in our lives.[5]

For your journal...

1. Jot down some practical steps you can take to let 'the word of Christ' dwell more richly in you.

2. Read again Jerry Bridges' account of buying bread. Select an ordinary part of your life. Describe how you can bring glory to God in that situation.

Colossians 3:23-24

And whatever you do, do it heartily, as to the Lord and not to men, knowing that from the Lord you will receive the reward of the inheritance; for you serve the Lord Christ.

Day 20
The Christian at Home and at Work

- *Begin by reading Colossians 3:18-4:1*
- *Pray about what you have read*
- *Make notes on what you think God is teaching you*
- *Read the following chapter*
- *Answer the questions in the 'For your journal' section*

Harold K. Moulton writes: 'Christian thinking has not become really Christian until it operates in our daily practice with those nearest to us.'[1]

Those nearest to us, of course, are our own family members and those with whom we work. Paul now turns to deal with the responsibility of the Christian in these areas.

The Christian at home (vv. 18-21)

Home life gives each Christian the opportunity to win many victories for Christ and his kingdom. If we are to secure these victories, we must have a clear and keen view of what we are trying to accomplish in our homes. If we aim for nothing, we are bound to hit it. The goal of the Christian home is to bring honour to God by modelling his grace and obeying his commandments.

We must also realize that this goal is attainable only if we use those means that God has appointed for godly living in the family: the Word of God, prayer and faithfulness to the house of God.

In short bursts Paul presents the duties of wives, husbands, children and parents.

Wives

Paul urges Christian wives to 'submit' to their husbands because this is 'fitting in the Lord'.

The word 'submit' is very unpopular. Few words have more power to enrage and infuriate. It is taken to mean that the woman is inferior. Nothing could be farther from the truth. In 1 Corinthians 11:3, Paul writes: 'But I want you to know that the head of every man is Christ, the head of woman is man, and the head of Christ is God.'

The key phrase in that verse is 'the head of Christ is God.' The Bible teaches that Christ was fully God in every respect (John 14:9-10). Why then would Paul say that God is 'head' of Christ? He is not suggesting that Christ was inferior to God as a person. He is talking rather about function. To provide salvation for sinners, it was necessary for Jesus to voluntarily submit himself to the Father.

The submission of the Christian wife is to be like Christ's. It is to be the voluntary submission of an equal for the purpose of achieving a noble end. In the case of the wife that noble end is the smooth functioning of the home.

Charles Erdman notes: 'In such submission there is nothing humiliating or degrading. It is not inconsistent with intellectual and moral and spiritual equality. It is merely the recognition of an authority which is essential to social and domestic order and welfare. It is the natural expression of love which manifests itself in willing service and finds joy in giving pleasure.'[2]

Husbands

Lest his readers think that the submission of Christian wives opens the door for their husbands to act as tyrants, the apostle quickly adds that husbands are to love their wives. In his letter to the Ephesians, Paul lifts this love to an even higher plane. He says: 'Husbands, love your wives, just as Christ also loved the church' (Eph. 5:25).

Those who think the apostle puts the heavier burden on the wife have not sufficiently pondered those words. Christ loved the church so strongly that he sacrificed himself on her behalf. Of this we can be sure — any husband who sincerely seeks to love his wife as Christ loved the church will find that she will have little trouble with submission.

Erdman says such love '...removes from the submission expected of a wife all that is distasteful or difficult. Indeed it places a husband in a position of actual subjection, for he is compelled by love to obey every claim the wife may make for support, for sympathy, for protection, for happiness.'[3]

This kind of love also makes it impossible for the husband to be 'bitter,' that is, insensitive and unkind, toward his wife.

Children

It is important to note that Paul begins his discussion of the home with the husband and the wife. He puts the marital relationship over the parental. We have a tendency to do the reverse. Paul had it right. If the marital relationship is what it is supposed to be, the children themselves will be enormously helped.

What duty does Paul assign children? He answers in these words: 'obey your parents in all things, for this is well pleasing to God.'

Some read these words and wonder if the apostle means that children are to obey when their parents require them to do things that are wrong. We must keep in mind that Paul is dealing only with the Christian home. Christian parents will not require un-Christian behaviour from their children.

Fathers

Paul addresses fathers because he expected them to take the lead in setting the rules and in providing discipline.

The apostle makes it obvious that Christian fathers are not to be heavy-handed and tyrannical. He recognizes that children can easily be discouraged and crushed by unreasonable demands and calls for their fathers to recognize the same. As we noted above concerning husbands, so we can note here that Christian fathers will conduct themselves in a way that will make them want to obey.

Peter Jeffrey identifies the following as exasperating conduct on the part of fathers:

- Over-protecting children as much as neglecting them
- Inconsistency in the father's life, where he is one thing at church and another at home
- Failure to let children grow up, and particularly in the teen years, to develop their own convictions
- Trying to relive his own childhood through his son.[4]

The Christian at work (3:22-4:1)

We may be inclined to think that what Paul says regarding the relationship of servants and masters has no value for us since the elimination of slavery. But the teachings here have on-going validity if we think of them in terms of the employee and employer relationship.

By the way, Scripture nowhere condones slavery. The apostle's instruction at this point was designed to deal with the situation that existed at that time. Paul refused to attack the institution and call for direct political action against it because he undoubtedly had confidence that the spreading of the gospel would finally eliminate it.

While we Christians are called to be good citizens and to exercise our political rights, we must not expect the evils of this world to be removed through political means. A better world calls for better people, and better people can be produced only by the life-changing power of the gospel of Christ.

Martyn Lloyd-Jones writes: 'It was the world that took eighteen centuries to see the wrongness of slavery, not the Christian teaching. The Christian teaching realizes that it cannot transform society as a whole; it must go on trusting that gradually the teaching will act as a leaven, and that men will become more and more enlightened. The time-lag is not to be explained in terms of the failure of biblical teaching; it is to be explained in terms of the blindness of the world to Christian teaching.'[5]

Servants

Paul called for Christian slaves to go about their work in such a way that it would be apparent to their masters that the gospel of Christ had caused a profound change in them. They were to do this in the following ways:

- by remembering that their masters were 'according to the flesh', that is, that they now had a higher master, the Lord Jesus Christ. They were, therefore, to view their service to their earthly masters as a means by which to serve their heavenly master. Whatever they did was to be done 'heartily, as to the Lord, and not to men' (v. 23).

• by serving without 'eyeservice, as men-pleasers'. In other words, they were not to do their work grudgingly, constantly looking to see if they were being watched and working diligently only if they were. They were rather to serve with 'sincerity of heart,' truly desiring to be of help to their masters and wanting to see their masters' enterprises succeed.

• by serving with the awareness that their true reward would eventually come from God (v. 24). Paul calls that reward 'the inheritance', that is, their inheritance in heaven. Slaves who had no earthly possessions had to rejoice in the promise that they would someday possess heaven.

On the other hand, Christian slaves were to keep in mind that wrong-doing would result in punishment (v. 25). They were not to think that their low status in life justified their wrong-doing.

Masters

The Apostle Paul did not want Christian masters to think that the responsibility for proper behaviour belonged only to their slaves. They were to also demonstrate that their lives had been changed by the gospel by treating their slaves justly and fairly and by remembering that God himself was the master to whom they would eventually answer.

Paul's words to servants and masters put before us two realities that we often forget: 1. Every-day life affords us many opportunities to advance the gospel of Christ. 2. It is not necessary to speak to advance the gospel. The attitude and spirit with which we go about our daily lives ought to make us stand out.

For your journal...

1. What are some ways that you can improve in your God-given role as a spouse?

2. Identify some ways in which you show on your job that you belong to Christ.

Colossians 4:5

Walk in wisdom toward those who are outside, redeeming the time.

Day 21
The Christian and Unbelievers

- *Begin by reading Colossians 4:2-6*
- *Pray about what you have read*
- *Make notes on what you think God is teaching you*
- *Read the following chapter*
- *Answer the questions in the 'For your journal' section*

In the last half of his letter, the apostle Paul quickly shifts from one arena of Christian responsibility to the other. He moves from the Christian's personal life to his church life to his home life. The one thing that remains unchanged in this shifting is exhortation. He continues throughout to lay before his readers the priority of appropriate Christian conduct.

The arena in the verses before us is the unbelieving world, or, to use Paul's phrase, 'those who are outside' (v. 5).

The mere mention of outsiders ought to lead each Christian to some soul-searching. Are we living with the awareness that we are on display? Do we frequently remind ourselves that unbelievers are not only observing us but also forming opinions and conclusions about Christianity on the basis of what they see in us? It is a solemn thing to ponder that many of those who are on the outside are there because of what they see from those who are on the inside.

Every Christian is at all times a witness to Christ. The only question is whether he or she is a good witness or a bad one.

Paul urges his readers to discharge three responsibilities as they keep outsiders in mind.

'Continue earnestly in prayer' (vv. 2-4)

A general call

The apostle begins this section with a general call for prayer. Each part of this call is significant and probing.

- 'Continue' means we are not to let up or relax in prayer. The Bible consistently reminds us of the need to be persistent and constant in prayer (Matt. 6:7-11; Eph. 6:18; 1 Thess. 5:17). The Lord Jesus himself 'spoke a parable,' the parable of the unjust judge, to make the point that 'men always ought to pray and not lose heart' (Luke 18:1).

- 'earnestly' means our praying is not to be the mere mouthing of words. True prayer has sweat on its brow and grime on its hands. It is to be fervent and intense.

- 'being vigilant' means we are to be watchful and on guard against everything that would hinder us. We are to be ever ready to beat back all distractions. We can rest assured that Satan understands far better than we the value of prayer and will oppose us in every way possible.

- 'with thanksgiving' means we are to be grateful that God has made us his children and given us the opportunity to pray and we are to verbally express this gratitude. Thanksgiving is the fuel in the tank of prayer.

A particular call

Having urged the Colossians to embrace the general duty of prayer, Paul now directs them to pray specifically for his success in the preaching of the gospel. He was not in doubt about the nature of the task to which he had been called. It was to make 'manifest' (v. 4) 'the mystery of Christ' (v. 3).

We think of a mystery as a dilemma that is solved by human perseverance and intellect. The word means something quite different in the Bible. It refers to truth that is inaccessible to the unaided human mind. It is truth that has to be revealed or it would not be known. The mystery of Christ refers to the truth of the gospel. God's way of saving sinners is a mystery. It consists of the second person of the Trinity taking our humanity and dying on a Roman cross. Who would have thought of such a plan? It seems utterly absurd. But this is God's way of salvation, and this was the message Paul had been called to make plain.

Declaring this message is no small challenge. People do not like to be told that they are sinners and in need of a Saviour. They do not like to hear a plan of salvation that seems so odd and peculiar. They do not like to be told that this alone is the way of salvation.

It is no wonder, then, that Paul felt the need for prayer. Paul was 'in chains' (v. 3) because of hostility to this kind of preaching. But those chains could not diminish his enthusiasm for the gospel. He does not ask that the Colossians pray for his release but rather that he use the opportunity provided by those chains to preach even more.

Paul's urgent request for prayer shows us that preaching is not something for which preachers alone are responsible. Preaching can only be effective and powerful if it is supported by the prayers of God's people. Christians cannot claim to have fulfilled their responsibilities to outsiders if they are not supporting through earnest prayer the preaching of the gospel of Christ.

'Walk in wisdom' (v. 5)

These words constitute the apostle's second exhortation. With the phrase 'walk in wisdom,' he was affirming that they were to conduct themselves in such a way to promote and further the gospel.

Part of walking in wisdom is 'redeeming the time,' that is, seizing every opportunity to speak for Christ. 'Redeeming' means 'buying up.' They were, then, to 'buy up' opportunities to share the gospel. William Hendriksen explains: 'The sense then would be 'Do not just sit there and wait for opportunity to fall into your lap, but go after it. Yes, buy it.'[1]

The believer in Christ is not to view his time in this world as nothing more than something to be experienced. He rather sees it as something to be used. He is to approach each day by asking how he can use it to bring glory to his Lord, to influence unbelievers for Christ and to sustain a good conscience before the Lord.

The apostle himself serves as the best example of this. As we have noted, he looked upon his imprisonment as an opportunity to further the gospel (see also Phil. 1:12).

Do we go about our business each day with the intent of creating openings to share the gospel? Do we view each situation in which we find ourselves — perhaps even a hospital! — as the opportunity to witness for Christ?

'Let your speech always be with grace' (v. 6)

Many passages of Scripture emphasize the importance of the Christian's speaking. The Lord Jesus stressed it during his earthly ministry. Our words, according to him, are not just from the mouth out. They are from the heart out, that is, our words accurately reflect our spiritual condition (Matt. 12:33-35). Jesus also indicated that our words will be minutely judged (Matt. 12:36-37).

The best known Scripture on this matter of speaking comes from James. He shows how easy it is for us to control horses and ships and to tame various wild beasts, but how difficult it is for us to control and tame the tongue. He calls it an 'unruly evil, full of deadly poison' (James 3:1-12).

In the verse before us, the apostle Paul adds his voice to Jesus' and James'. He tells us what should be present in Christian speaking. He writes: 'Let your speech always be with grace, seasoned with salt, that you may know how you ought to answer each one' (Col. 4:6).

First, our speech is to be filled with 'grace.' John MacArthur writes: 'To speak with grace means to say what is spiritual, wholesome, fitting, kind, sensitive, purposeful, complementary, gentle, truthful, loving, and thoughtful.'[2]

Secondly, our speech is to be 'seasoned with salt'. Salt is a preservative. It keeps decay from setting in. MacArthur says: 'Believers' speech should act as a purifying influence, rescuing conversation from the filth that so often engulfs it.'[3]

Nothing is more common than excusing unhelpful, unwholesome speech by pointing to the stress created by difficult circumstances. It's easy to justify rotten speech by pointing to our children, our spouse, the boss, the neighbors, and so on.

But Paul does not say we are to speak wholesome words only when everything in life is peachy. If this were the case, we would never speak wholesome words. No, Paul says 'always'. And what-

ever our circumstances, our speech is to remain free from rottenness and full of grace.

We may think the apostle would not say such a thing today, that his command was given to tranquil people who lived in
tranquil times. Today's Christians seem to think they are the first
ones to ever experience stress in life. But the early Christians
to whom Paul wrote probably had more stress than we will ever
have. In addition to not having all the conveniences that make
our lives comfortable, they often found themselves facing severe
persecution for their faith.

*No part of life gives us a greater opportunity to demonstrate
the difference Christ has made in us than our speech. J.C.
Ryle writes: 'There is nothing, perhaps, to which most men
pay less attention than their words.'⁴*

*But the Christian is not to be classified with most men.
He has been dramatically changed, and, because of that, he
should evidence a deep concern that his words be clean and
pure. Someone has observed that the Christian should speak
in such a way that he wouldn't be afraid to sell his parrot to
the town gossip.*

For your journal...

1. What is your response to Paul's description of prayer? How does your prayer life measure up? What can you do to improve in this area?

2. Think about how you use your time. Write down ways in which you can use it more wisely.

3. Think about your speech. What steps can you take to improve in this area?

Colossians 4:18

This salutation by my own hand — Paul. Remember my chains. Grace be with you. Amen.

Day 22
Closing Thoughts

- *Begin by reading Colossians 4:7-18*
- *Pray about what you have read*
- *Make notes on what you think God is teaching you*
- *Read the following chapter*
- *Answer the questions in the 'For your journal' section*

Those who prize the writings of Paul know that his closing words should not be ignored. They invariably contain gems of comfort and instruction. They remind us that Paul was not writing doctrinal essays detached from life. He was always writing as a pastor with the spiritual welfare of his people in mind, and the doctrine with which he invariably begins his letters is essential for the well-being of his readers.

The closing verses of Colossians brim with warmth. We can divide them into the following: the messengers of Paul, the companions of Paul, the instructions of Paul and the salutation of Paul.

The messengers of Paul (vv. 7-9)

The apostle could not close his letter without expressing sincere appreciation and warm approval of his closest associates and coworkers. The greatness of a man can be measured to some degree by his ability to attract and inspire others. Paul was a monumental man who either drew from others deep devotion or fierce hatred. Charles Erdman writes: 'The names of the friends grouped around that of the apostle form a brilliant galaxy, shining like stars around a central sun.'[1]

Tychicus

Tychicus was one of Paul's closest and most trusted associates. A native of Asia Minor, he accompanied Paul on his third missionary journey (Acts 20:4). He was now to bear the apostle's letter to the Colossians, to report on Paul's condition, to learn about the circumstances of the Colossians so he could in return report to Paul and to provide comfort for the believers in Colosse.

Paul commends Tychicus as 'a beloved brother, a faithful minister, and a fellow servant in the Lord'.

'Beloved brother' reminds us of warmth of the relationship created by the gospel of Christ. Christians are not merely associated with each other because of common interests and objectives. They are bound to each other by a common life.

The term 'faithful minister' indicates that Tychicus found happiness in doing whatever was necessary to advance the work of the Lord. He did not desire prominence or fame.

The phrase 'fellow servant in the Lord' tells us that Tychicus and Paul were not only bound together by the warmth of brotherhood but also by the industry of servanthood. We can rest assured that both men counted it a privilege to serve the Lord together. Their example of servanthood urges us to be diligent in our service to the Lord while we can. Christians will be brothers and sisters in Christ forever, but they can be fellow-servants in the church only for a brief time.

Onesimus

Onesimus, the subject of Paul's brief letter to Philemon, was a slave who had run away from his master, encountered the apostle Paul who led him to the knowledge of Christ. Paul was now sending him with Tychicus to Colosse as 'a faithful and beloved brother.'

> *We surely cannot read the apostle's words about Tychicus and Onesimus without admiring again the power of the gospel to take diverse people and weld them into a unity of spirit and effort. With Paul, Tychicus and Onesimus, the gospel had overcome the natural divisions of Jew and Gentile, free and slave to create a warm-hearted brotherhood. One of the best ways we can witness to the life-changing power of the gospel is by displaying sincere love for our brothers and sisters in Christ of all walks and stations of life.*

The companions of Paul (vv. 10-15)

Three comforting companions

In these verses the apostle sends greeting to the Colossians on behalf of three Jewish converts who had been 'a comfort' during his imprisonment (v. 11):

Aristarchus (v. 10). Paul's fellow-prisoner, Aristarchus was a convert from Thessalonica and a frequent companion. He was with the apostle when the riot broke out in Ephesus (Acts 19:29). He accompanied Paul on his final journey to Jerusalem, where the apostle was arrested and transported first to Caesarea and then to Rome. He

was with Paul on the stormy and frightening voyage from
Caesarea to Rome (Acts 27:2).

Mark (v. 10). Mark, who would eventually author the
gospel that bears his name, was also with the apostle at
this time and sent his greetings as well. The apostle here
identifies Mark only as 'the cousin of Barnabas' (v. 10).
He could also have identified him as the man who had
forsaken him and Barnabas on their first missionary journey, a disappointment so bitter for Paul that it caused him
and Barnabas to go their separate ways when he, Paul, refused to take Mark on his second missionary journey.

Paul and Mark were eventually reconciled, and Paul
asked Mark to come and minister to him during his imprisonment. Paul makes reference to instructions the
Colossians had received about Mark (v. 10). Charles Erdman explains this reference in this way: 'What these
commandments were and when sent cannot be conjec-
tured unless the meaning is that the commandments
were that, as stated, Mark should be cordially received
should he visit the Colossian church. The implication is
that Mark's early failure may have been known in Colosse
and prejudice against him still may have been felt.'[2]

Jesus who is called Justus (v. 11). This man is mentioned
nowhere else in Paul's writings. His Jewish name, Jesus
or Joshua, was not unusual. It was a common practice
at that time for Jews to add a Greek name to their given
Jewish name. Hence Jesus became known as Justus.

Additional companions (vv. 12-14)

Paul here names three additional companions who desired to
send their greetings to the church.

Epaphras (vv. 12-13). Hailing from Colosse, Epaphras was converted to Christ during Paul's ministry in Ephesus. He had reported to Paul the false teaching that was troubling the church. He desired to see the church 'stand perfect and complete in all the will of God' (v. 12), and he prayed fervently to that end.

Epaphras coupled with his concern for the church in Colosse an intense interest for the neighbouring cities of Laodicea and Hierapolis (v. 13).

What a rare man he was! The wonderful traits of zeal for the truth, diligence in prayer and fervour for evangelism blended in his heart in an admirable way.

Luke (v. 14). Known as the 'beloved physician,' Luke frequently travelled with Paul and was well-known to all who knew the apostle. He needed nothing more, therefore, than mere mention.

Demas (v. 14). As Luke's name is associated with faithfulness to Paul, Demas has become associated with faithlessness. The reason for this is Paul's cryptic words in his second letter to Timothy: 'Demas has forsaken me, having loved this present world' (2 Tim. 4:10).

Paul had a tremendous capacity for friendship. He loved people of all kinds and by his selflessness and devotion to Christ drew from them faithful and diligent ministry. We should strive to set an example of devotion to Christ that others will want to follow. And in these times in which people are so easily enamoured with movie stars, singers and athletes, we should always remember that the true heroes will prove to be ordinary folks who extraordinarily gave themselves in service to the Lord.

The instructions of Paul (vv. 16-17)

After sharing the greetings of those with him, Paul proceeded to give the Colossians some instructions. He wanted the Colossians to send this letter on to Laodicea. False teaching knows no bounds, and Paul did not want the truth he had written to be restricted to Colosse. He had also written a letter to the church in Laodicea which would eventually arrive in Colosse. He wanted that letter read aloud in the Colossian church. This letter has been lost.

Paul also gives the church some instructions regarding Archippus, whom we also find mentioned in the apostle's letter to Philemon (v. 2). The instructions here cause us to assume that he needed some encouragement in discharging the gospel ministry to which he had been called. Paul exhorts the church to provide this (v. 17).

> *Paul's instructions to the church about Archippus remind us of the gift, the goal and the guard of the ministry. The gift is that the call comes from the Lord. The goal is to fulfil or complete that to which the Lord has called. The guard is taking heed. Only by being watchful and prayerful can the minister effectively guard against the many dangers that attend the ministry. These words also indicate that there is much churches can and should do to encourage those who have been called to the gospel ministry.*

The salutation of Paul (v. 18)

These words indicate that one of Paul's associates actually penned his words up to this point. The apostle himself then took the pen and signed his name and wrote: 'Remember my chains. Grace be with you. Amen.'

His request that they remember his imprisonment should probably not be taken as a plea for sympathy. It is rather his way of reminding his readers that the truth of the gospel, which he so vigorously advances in this letter, is not something that he took lightly. It was for this truth that he was in chains.

His fervent devotion to the gospel constitutes a ringing call to all of us to be fervent in our devotion as well.

For your journal...

1. Make a list of faithful friends and companions who have brought blessing into your life. Give thanks to God for them.

2. What does Paul's ability to inspire others to diligent service tell you about him? What can you do to inspire others to serve Christ?

3. Tychicus was frequently sent on special missions by Paul. Read Ephesians 6:21-22, 2 Timothy 4:12. What kind of disposition does it take to do the kind of work Tychicus did?

4. What does the mention of Mark tell you about the apostle Paul? Did he practice forgiveness? What does the apostle Paul teach about forgiveness? Read Ephesians 4:32.

Notes

Day 1 - Introduction
1. Michael Bentley, *The Guide: Colossians & Philemon,* Evangelical Press, p.15.
2. Herbert M. Carson, *Tyndale New Testament Commentaries: The Epistles of Paul to the Colossians and Philemon,* Wm. B. Eerdmans Publishing Company, p.17.

Day 2 - Affection for the Church
1. John Gill, *Exposition of the Old & New Testaments,* The Baptist Standard Bearer, Inc., vol. ix, p.376).

Day 3 – Thanksgiving for the Gospel
1. William Hendriksen, *New Testament Commentary: Exposition of Colossians and Philemon.* Baker Book House, p.51.
2. As above.
3. As above.
4. Charles R. Erdman, *The Epistles of Paul to the Colossians and to Philemon,* The Westminster Press, p.39.
5. *The Bethany Parallel Commentary on the New Testament,* Bethany House Publishers, p.1181.

Day 4 - A Prayer of Intercession
1. *Bethany Parallel Commentary,* p.1181.
2. Hendriksen, *Commentary,* p.56.

3. Cited by Geoffrey B. Wilson, *Colossians and Philemon: A Digest of Reformed Comment*, The Banner of Truth Trust, p.23.
4. Hendriksen, *Commentary*, p.57.
5. Richard Lenski, *The Interpretation of St. Paul's Epistles to the Colossians, to the Thessalonians, to Timothy, to Titus and to Philemon*, Augsburg Publishing House, p.34.
6. from Isaac Watts' hymn *Am I a Soldier of the Cross*.
7. Hendriksen, *Commentary*, p.58.

Day 5 – Thanksgiving for Salvation
1. Erdman, *Colossians*, p.43.
2. cited by Wilson, *Colossians*, p.26.
3. Lenski, *Colossians*, p.39.

Day 6 – The Supremacy of Christ
1. Warren Wiersbe, *The Bible Exposition Commentary*, Victor Books, vol. ii, p.114.
2. Clinton E. Arnold, *Zondervan Illustrated Bible Backgrounds Commentary*, Zondervan, vol. iii, p.379.
3. Gerhard Kittel, ed., *Theological Dictionary of the New Testament*, Wm. B. Eerdmans Publishing Company, vol. ii, p.389.
4. Hendriksen, *Commentary*, p.76.
5. Erdman, *Colossians*, pp.48-9.
6. R. Kent Hughes, *Preaching the Word: Colossians and Philemon*, Crossway Books, p.34.

Day 7 – The Fullness of Christ
1. Wilson, *Colossians*, p.35.
2. Charles R. Erdman, *The Gospel of Matthew*, The Westminster Press, p.136.
3. Max Anders, *Holman New Testament Commentary: Galatians, Ephesians, Philippians & Colossians*, Broadman & Holman Publishers, vol. viii, p.287.

4. R.C. Lucas, *The Message of Colossians & Philemon*, Inter-Varsity Press, p.59.
5. As above, p. 55.

Day 8 – The Riches of Reconciliation
1. Hendriksen, *Commentary*, p.82.
2. Wilson, *Colossians*, p.37.

Day 10 – Diligence in Ministry
1. Cited by Curtis Vaughn, *A Study Guide: Colossians*, Zondervan Publishing House, p.54.
2. Hendriksen, *Commentary*, pp.88-9.
3. Lenski, *Colossians*, p.79.

Day 11 – Diligence in Intercession
1. Erdman, *Colossians*, p.61.
2. Hendriksen, *Commentary*, p.104.

Day 12 – Wise Words for Pressured Believers
1. *New Geneva Study Bible*, Thomas Nelson Publishers, p.1884.
2. Arnold, *Commentary*, pp.384-5
3. Erdman, *Colossians*, p.68.

Day 13 – The Sufficiency of Christ
1. F.F. Bruce, *The New International Commentary on the New Testament: Colossians*, Wm. B. Eerdmans Publishing, p.167.
2. As above.
3. John MacArthur, *The MacArthur New Testament Commentary: Colossians & Philemon*, p.107.
4. As above.
5. R.C. Sproul, *Saved from What?*, Crossway Books, pp.83-4.
6. Lenski, *Colossians*, p.104.

Day 14 – Completeness in Christ
1. Cited by Wilson, *Colossians*, p.54.
2. Vaughn, *Colossians*, p.75.
3. John Flavel, *The Works of John Flavel*, The Banner of Truth Trust, vol. i, p.437.
4. Wilson, *Colossians*, p.56.
5. Bruce, *Colossians*, p.242.

Day 15 – 'Therefore'
1. Lucas, *Colossians*, pp.111-2.
2. Wilson, *Colossians*, p.57.
3. Lucas, *Colossians*, p.114.
4. As above, p.115.
5. As above, p.124.
6. Cited by Frederick S. Leahy, *The Cross He Bore*, The Banner of Truth Trust, p.81.

Day 16 – Looking to Things Above
1. Lucas, *Colossians*, p.132.
2. As above, p.135.
3. D.M. Lloyd-Jones, *Romans: An Exposition of Chapter 6*, Zondervan Publishing House, p.107.
4. Wilson, *Colossians*, p.65.
5. Bruce, *Colossians*, p.257.
6. Lucas, *Colossians*, p.140.
7. Gill, *Exposition*, p.197.

Day 17 – Dealing With Things Below
1. Matthew Henry, *Matthew Henry's Commentary on the Whole Bible*, Fleming H. Revell Company, vol. vi, p.614.
2. Erdman, *Colossians*, p.82.
3. MacArthur, *Colossians*, p.152.

Day 18 – What to Put On
1. Wilson, *Colossians*, pp.73-4.
2. Erdman, *Colossians*, p.87.

Day 19 – Letting and Doing
1. Gill, *Exposition*, p.202.
2. Vaughn, *Colossians*, p.102.
3. Bruce, *Colossians*, p.286.
4. Jerry Bridges, *I Give You Glory, O God*, Waterbrook Press, pp.13-4.
5. As above, p. 14.

Day 20 – The Christian at Home and at Work
1. Cited by Vaughn, *Colossians*, p.104.
2. Erdman, *Colossians*, p.94.
3. As above.
4. Peter Jeffrey, *Opening up Ephesians*, Solid Ground Christian Books, p.68.
5. D.M. Lloyd-Jones, *Life in the Spirit*, Baker Book House, p.337.

Day 21 – The Christian and Unbelievers
1. Hendriksen, *Commentary*, pp.182-3.
2. MacArthur, *Colossians*, p.187.
3. As above.
4. J.C. Ryle, *Expository Thoughts on Matthew*, The Banner of Truth Trust, p.132.

Day 22 – Closing Thoughts
1. Erdman, *Colossians*, p.101.
2. As above, p.106.

Publishing With a Mission

A wide range of excellent books on spiritual subjects is available from Evangelical Press. Please write to us for your free catalogue or contact us by e-mail. Full details are also available on our web site.

Evangelical Press
Faverdale North Industrial Estate, Darlington, Co. Durham, DL3 0PH, England

Evangelical Press USA
P. O. Box 825, Webster, New York 14580, USA

e-mail: sales@evangelicalpress.org

web: http://www.evangelicalpress.org